39 MONTHS

39 MONTHS
WITH THE "TIGERS," 1915-1918

BY

D. V. KELLY, M.C.

(formerly Captain, Leicestershire Regiment)

LONDON
Ernest Benn Limited

First Published in
1930

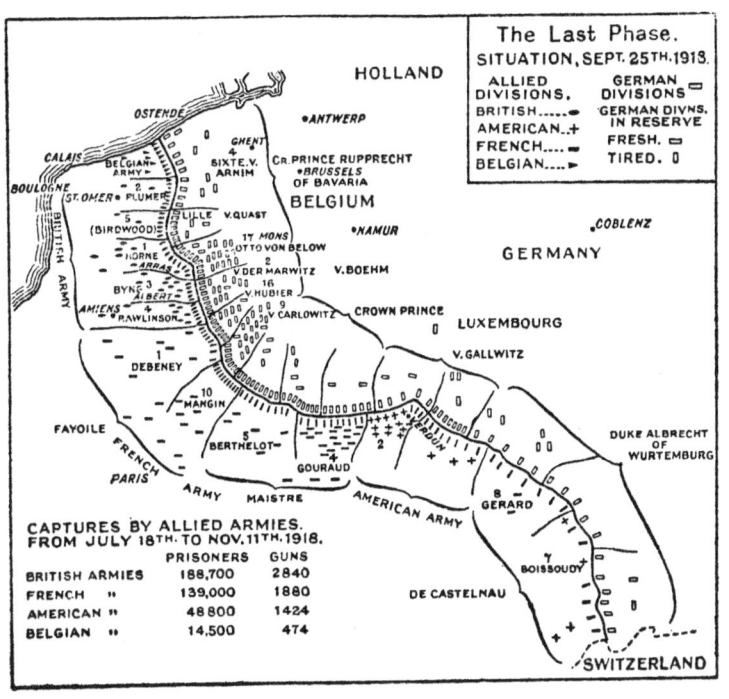

PREFACE

WHY ANOTHER WAR BOOK?

A SELECTION of descriptive comments on the War, ranging over the period from 1914 to the present year, would produce a remarkably confused picture of the British soldier. It would start presumably with the war-time journalist's creation of the " cheerful, laughing Tommy ", who apparently spent his time alternately singing " Tipperary ", or chasing the flying enemy with loud shouts of " Avenge the *Lusitania !* ". Then would come—after a short spasm of mostly excellent narratives which found few readers—a period of ten years' silence when " the public didn't want to hear about the War "—and then——! " This," says a reviewer of a recent war-book, " is the same old story of mud and vermin : filth and gore : of once bright hopes steeped in comrades' blood : of a tottering faith in God and a vague distrust of mankind." " Strewth ! " as the victims would have said—gone is the " cheerful, laughing " fantasy of the journalists, to be replaced by a drunken savage, incapable of any conversation except blasphemy and profanity, of any ideals beyond a hope of a " cushy " wound !

This flood of pornography makes one sit up and think. Were we all really such sub-human brutes as we appear in some of the war-books? Did we lose faith in God and man? Were our bright hopes steeped in comrades' gore? Did we think of nothing but drink and fornication? Were we deluded into enlisting by politicians, and did elementary patriotism have nothing to do with it merely because we did not talk about it? To judge by the reception given to this kind of war-book, many people seem to think so. I gravely doubt whether the normal ex-Service man subscribes to this view. Units differed of course, but I honestly believe that not one per cent. of my old Brigade bore the least resemblance either to the war-time journalist's caricature, or to the rather conceited neurotic individual who appears likely to pass into popular legend as the type of the British Army in the Great War.

This little narrative was written in the spring of 1919, without thought of publication, and would probably never have seen the light had not the sudden revival of interest in war-literature tempted me to dig it out and re-examine it. Though only too well aware of the absence of picturesque or sensational elements, I feel that perhaps the consecutive story of the sacrifices and successes of one unit right through its war career, written by an eye-witness, in the full atmosphere of the period, and from a memory then perfectly fresh and clear, might conceivably have a certain limited appeal.

PREFACE   ix

It is just possible that the very absence of all propaganda for any " ism " may serve as a reminder of that concentration of interest on the work in hand, that absorption in the events of the moment, which during nearly five years obliterated among millions of British soldiers all feeling of civilian class-distinction and money-distinction, and produced the extraordinary sense of freemasonry unique in our history, and now perhaps only surviving wherever ex-Service men meet with no outsiders present?

And so, with a very few retouches, such as the allusions in Chapter V to " Journey's End " I offer this little book, with apologies for its dryness and other imperfections, to the few whom it may interest.

CONTENTS

Preface—Why Another War Book? . . . . PAGE 7

CHAPTER
I. "Peace Warfare" 15
II. The Somme 25
III. Arras—1916 35
IV. The Somme Once More . . 43
V. Mud: The Hohenzollern Redoubt in 1916-17 . . 50
VI. The Hindenburg Line . . 58
VII. The Bloody Salient (Ypres 1917) 73
VIII. Waiting for the March Offensive 86
IX. March, 1918 95
X. April, 1918 110
XI. May, 1918 121
XII. The Last Interval . . . 133
XIII. The Beginning of the End . 136
XIV. The Last Phase . . . 148

ILLUSTRATIONS

Cartoon by Leon Arnal . . .	*Frontispiece*
	TO FACE PAGE
Hohenzollern Redoubt shewing Fosse and Slag heap	51
A "Close-up" of Hindenburg Support line in front of Fontaine village	60
The Hindenburg Line at Fontaine-les-Croisilles, April, 1917, showing V shaped belts of barbed wire . .	61
Fontaine Village and Hindenburg Support Line	63
Fontaine-les-Croisilles from North-West side, attacked on May 3rd, 1917	65
The Épéhy Sector, Jan.-March, 1918. Left half of Sector. (Poplar Trench our front line.)	87
The Épéhy Sector, Jan.-March, 1918. Right half of Sector . . .	89

MAPS

The Last Phase, Situation Sept. 25, 1915	PAGE	VI
The Somme Battle Area		26
Arras, 1916		34
Montauban-Longueval-Flers Road	.	42
The Berles Sector and Hindenburg Line	.	59

MAPS

Hindenburg Line, May 1917 . . PAGE	62
The Ypres Salient, 1917-18 . . .	74
The March Retreat: The Advance Aug.-Oct., 1918	94
British Front Line: May 27th, 1918 . .	120
The Last Phase, Oct.-Nov. 1918 . .	149

THIRTY-NINE MONTHS

CHAPTER I

"PEACE WARFARE"

ON the night of the 29th July, 1915, the Infantry Brigade, to which this narrative is dedicated, arrived at Folkestone by train from a camp on Salisbury Plain, embarked and sailed from England in utter darkness and complete silence. It was oddly symbolical of the anonymous, untheatrical character of the Brigade's future career in France, a character which has always seemed to invest this last War with a special note of dramatic pathos, deeper than that of previous wars where the individual and the regiment received always some measure of recognition and moral support. As the crowded troopship moved off in the night I remembered the illustrations of fourteen years before, showing South African troopships lined by cheering soldiers waving to the bands and crowds ashore.

The 110th Infantry Brigade was composed of the 6th, 7th, 8th and 9th " Leicesters ", four battalions of keen and willing men—my own battalion had almost all joined in August, 1914—drawn mostly from the same district and fully up to strength. Within three years, despite constant reinforcements, there were only three battalions, all woefully under strength, and only two of these were of the Leicestershire Regiment.

In the early dawn we landed at Boulogne, marched to Ostrohove rest-camp, and from there by train to Houlle for a week's training in the forest of Eperlecques. More serious training followed with a week in the neighbourhood of Locre, a village a little south of Ypres, where detachments of the Brigade made their first acquaintance with the trenches, and I received my own " baptism of fire " during a first tour of the line, in the course of which exactly two bullets whined overhead. Perhaps no amount of subsequent experience can give the same thrill as the first exposure to fire, for nature, as the War so often proved, makes all things in time seem normal and stale. Otherwise, that first of many hundred trench-walks has left very little impression, and of all that week I retain chiefly the memory of swarms of greedy flies which haunted the filthy farm occupied by Brigade headquarters to which I had just been attached.

It was with great relief that after a train journey to Doullens and a two days' march via Mondicourt, we found ourselves in the pleasant undulating country south of Arras, with its green fields and clean villages, each set in its cluster of woods and orchards. Here the Brigade took over from the French Army the

Berles sector, a line of trenches running east of the villages of Berles and Bienvillers. Some hundreds of civilians still lived in these villages, although the communication trenches meandered back right into them and they were almost within machine-gun range of the enemy. Facing us was the ruined village of Monchy, which formed part of the German line, and a short way west of the Berles-Bienvillers road lay Pommier, the village where the Brigade headquarters settled.

I made a preliminary tour of the whole line with Taudières, a young French officer similarly attached to the headquarters of the French regiment we were relieving, and so received my first impression of the French at war, a spectacle which always fascinated me. Mr. Belloc remarks somewhere that a French farmer will plant thorns where an English farmer will spend £4 on a gate, and that both methods keep out cows, and I often had the same feeling about the two national methods of waging trench warfare. Visiting French trenches one was always struck by the superficial air of fraternity and negligence among all ranks. Officers gave one the impression of being elder brothers of the same family as the men, and comparatively little attention seemed to be given to appearances. To the casual eye sentries seemed slack and working parties rare. The impression was superficial only, but the same easy-going method applied in an English regiment might rapidly dissolve it into a mob.

Again, although the French were content with brushwood hurdles to hold up the sides of the trenches where we had solid wooden " V-frames ", and with casual bricks underfoot—or often nothing at all—where we floored every foot with wooden " duck-boards", our trenches had an unhappy knack of becoming neck-deep quagmires, often having to be practically abandoned, while theirs mostly held. According to one theory this was due to the light springy tread of the "*poilu*"—according to another, it was because the French did not use them so much. They were already attaching great faith to small isolated strong points—"*points d'appui*" or "*tenailles*", small self-contained labyrinths of trenches with their own garrisons. We adopted this policy before March, 1918, but it did not keep out Germans as effectively as the thorns keep out cows. Again, it was the French practice to " let sleeping dogs lie " when in a quiet sector and not actually contemplating an attack, and of making this clear by retorting vigorously only when challenged. In one sector which we took over from them they explained to me that they had practically a code which the enemy well understood : they fired two shots for each one that came over, but never fired first. Therein lay perhaps the most striking difference between our two armies.

Even the small point of trench-names yielded an amusing instance of the more light-hearted style in which the French Army made war. At Berles, for example, the French had officially baptized their own and the enemy trenches either with the names of prominent characters or, giving rein to the imagination, with such pleasing fancies as " *Boyau des Houris* " or " *Tranchée des* 1001 *délices* ". The English staff officer arrived on the scene and promptly devised a new list of names entirely beginning with the letter " N "—" Naked Street ", " Nawful Street ", etcetera. I suppose both systems were equally effective—or ineffective—in keeping enemies out.

My chief memory of that golden autumn and hard winter of 1915 in the trenches south of Arras is one of peace—peace that is in comparison with what came after. There was little shelling from either side (though enemy trench-mortar fire began to be annoying after November), trench raids had not become an obsession, and casualties were few except, in the depth of winter, from trench feet and trench fever. Before dawn each day I assembled the H.Q. personnel and marched or ran with them for a half hour along the roads behind the trenches, watching the picturesque fireworks of the Very lights along the line, and each morning rode with the Brigadier to one or other of our two villages, where we entered the communication trenches and set off for a tramp round the line.

When the real winter came this ceased to be amusing as it meant dragging oneself—encased in gumboots to the thigh—for several miles each way through waist-deep mud, and in many places the front line itself became pretty difficult. But the sector remained fundamentally peaceful, and all through that winter both the Brigade headquarters and the resting battalions slept comfortably in inhabited farmhouses though within a few thousand yards of the enemy. We actually organized in Bienvillers village itself a Brigade laundry, staffed by peasant-women, enabling the men to get frequent changes of underclothing, and once every week I sat in the improvised laundry and paid out wages to our laundresses.

In those happy days, we thought twenty rounds of gunfire to be a heavy bombardment, and when the battle of Loos was fought up north we were quite excited by the "coöperation" of our artillery to the extent, I fancy, of a hundred rounds in three days. General Snow, in whose corps we were, came to our headquarters to ask if all our transport were ready to move, crying in his enthusiasm " We've got 'em stone cold ! " Once I took a holiday in the form of a visit to my own old Company, then in the front line, and vastly enjoyed the hospitality of my own contemporaries. I went with the Company commander on an eerie walk in Nomansland—which was, however, about one hundred and fifty yards wide there—and inspected the bodies of a dozen or more French territorials, in the old pre-war uniforms, which had lain out there for perhaps a year close to a sunken road leading into the German-held village of Monchy Aux Bois. By some curious freak of nature one of them had been completely preserved as though turned to stone, with clearly marked features and a beard.

Casualties, as has been indicated, were relatively few in those days, and one was the more painfully impressed by the loss of the first officer from my own old battalion, Lieutenant Champneys, which had a curious sequel. Champneys had gone out on patrol during a fog, and with some presentiment had left all his personal effects behind. The fog lifted, and he remained out, wounded, and was taken prisoner. Soon after a German shouted across that he had died in Monchy. Nearly two years later we passed through Monchy in the wake of the Germans who were in retreat to the Hindenburg Line, and there I found his grave, inscribed with the date of the day he was captured, and the name of his regiment, and it is pleasant to say, as scrupulously kept as though in an English cemetery at home.

The only other impression of that winter worth recording was the sudden wave of enthusiasm for bombing which swept through our army, as a result of heavy losses sustained by the Guards in the Hohenzollern Redoubt in October. Every Brigade staff adopted a bombing officer, and our own had a school a hundred strong. For a time it became an article of faith that the Mills bomb was going to end the War, and when open warfare suddenly revived in the Great Attacks of 1918 it was found that the lesson had been learned only too well, and that the use of the rifle had been well-nigh forgotten.

In the spring of 1916 the 37th Division was relieved by the 4th—our own Brigade by an Irish one, the 10th.

After a few weeks out of the line we returned to an area on the right of our old sector, the new area including the ruins of the village of Hannescamps.

Looking back, I see those early summer months of 1916 as a kind of watershed between the old peaceful stalemate and the new aggressive activity on our side which set in with Verdun and the establishment of a continuous lavish flow of munitions and artillery from England. From June, 1916, until the end of the War there seemed to be a steadily increasing liveliness with the intervals of stagnancy growing ever shorter. It was about that time that we were joined by a machine gun company and a Stokes trench-mortar battery (belated replies to the German organization, which had enjoyed a long superiority in both those arms) but what was more significant was the appearance of our heavy artillery in ever-growing strength. The air was now full of rumours of the coming Somme offensive, and every week batteries of 6-inch, 60-pounders, 8-inch, 9·2's, and even 12-inch, kept arriving, taking up positions in the orchards and gardens surrounding the farms, mostly still inhabited.

Janelle, our interpreter, who had a taste for folklore, made the interesting discovery that the neighbourhood was honeycombed with old quaries entered usually from holes in the side of wells. Some of these were cleared and made accessible and one at least, near Bienvillers, used as an ammunition dump, but, in general, I fear that little use was made of this knowledge. The mention of folklore reminds me of a curious illustration of the strong traditional feeling of the French peasant. Janelle found that the farmers still pointed to certain cross country tracks leading to Bienvillers from several miles away as the daily itinerary of an Irish missionary who had lived about twelve centuries ago, along which were some old Calvaries which marked, it was said, the spots where he rested and prayed : while in Bienvillers itself an ancient stone was pointed out as the spot where he had said Mass, and this stone lay not in the vicinity of the modern church of Bienvillers, but in the disused yard of a church which had been destroyed at the time of the French Revolution. I commend this elaborate piece of tradition to those who imagine the French are merely revolutionaries.

Another incident comes to mind which illustrates another aspect of rural conservatism. Our Brigade headquarters had been all through the winter in a farm belonging to the maire of Pommier, who being maire had in the centre of his courtyard a dungheap larger than had any of his neighbours. After a while our Brigadier could stand this no longer, and not content with having the dungheap removed, had ten cartloads of bricks—the spoil of some ruin—brought to the farm and used to pave the whole yard. The maire, when I tried to console him by a glorious vision of a future without flies, assured me with the national logic that matters would be worse even in this respect as the flies would now come indoors, being deprived of their usual abode; and when many months later we again passed through Pommier I was not surprised to see the dungheap restored to its old situation.

CHAPTER II

THE SOMME

ON July 1st, 1916, the Brigade, now commanded by General Hessey, as General Bainbridge was gone to command a Division, was out of the line, concentrated round Humbercamp village in readiness to follow up the attack of the 46th and 56th Divisions at Gommecourt, on the extreme left of the Somme offensive. For several evenings immediately before the 1st of July we had watched the endless line of gunflashes and bursting shells, as our new heavy batteries pounded the German line from Fricourt to Gommecourt. All through the day of July 1st we were receiving conflicting reports of the progress of the attacks near us—first that the 56th Division had broken through south of Gommecourt, then that the 46th Division had failed to the north of it. One battalion was actually ordered up to Hebuterne, but was withdrawn. Then came sudden orders for our Brigade to march away independently to replace the 63rd Brigade of the 21st Division, badly cut up in the attack on Fricourt. We marched through Pas, where we saw for the last time the 37th Divisional staff, who were standing in front of their headquarters, neither did we ever see

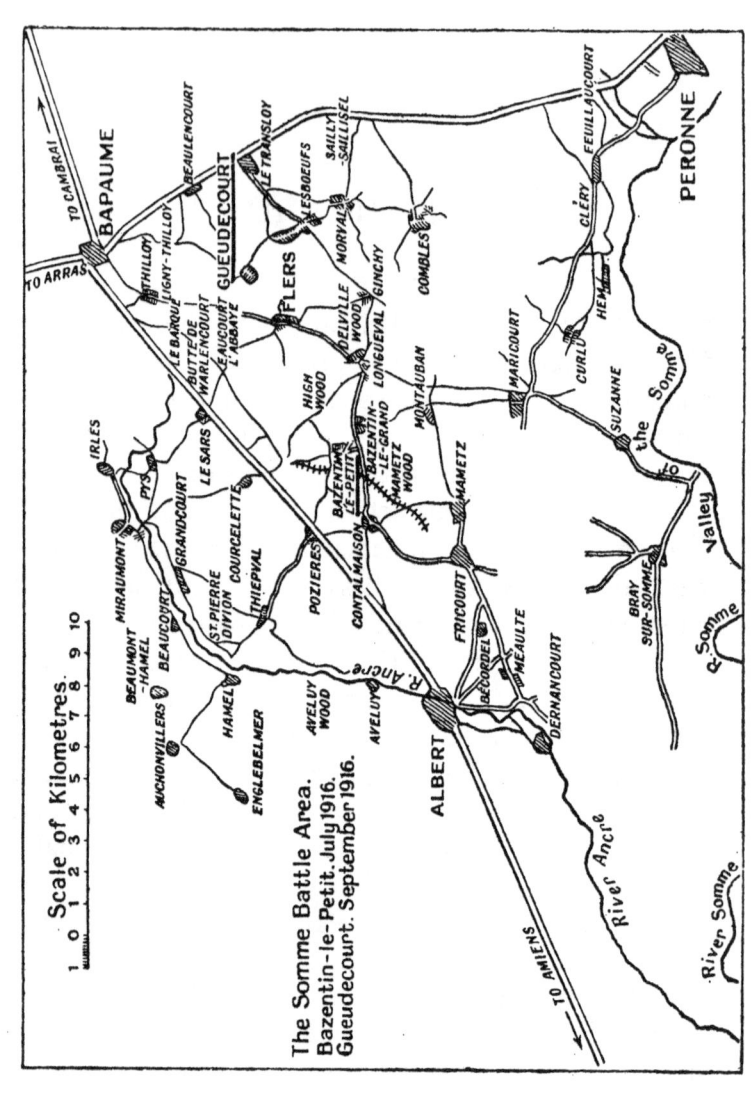

again our two other Brigades, and until the end of the War we were in the 21st Division with the 62nd and 64th Infantry Brigades.

It was a dismal march, for the roads were sodden with rain and the men in bad condition after a year's trench warfare and a bad winter, and mounted officers were busy riding back and forth collecting stragglers. At Talmas, our first stop, Colonel Ricardo, of the Inniskilling Fusiliers, called on our new Brigadier, and we heard from him the moving tale of the fruitless heroism of his Ulstermen (36th Division) at Serre on July 1st. After a day or more at Hangest we entrained for a camp and from there marched to Méaulte, the first of the untidy Somme villages we were destined to encounter, with their inhospitable peasants, who contrasted sadly with the cheery farmers of the Arras country. I remember vividly our failure to borrow a room for a Commanding Officer's Conference on the eve of our attack. That same night, however, we marched along the Albert road to Fricourt (which had been captured on the 1st of July), and the battalions took over some recently German trenches north-east of Fricourt Wood, between Contalmaison and Mametz.

The Brigade headquarters took over a great German dugout—the first of the kind we had seen—with three stories, beneath the site of Fricourt Château. The dugout—which contained hundreds of beds, and had been fitted with electric light—was naturally not forgotten by the German artillery, and I remember the unfortunate carrier-pigeons, cage and all, being blown down the entrance staircase. This was about July 10th, and on the next day I went round the line with Hinkley the Brigade bombing officer. Now for the first time I saw what was to become only too familiar a sight—trenches heaped with dead (mostly, I think, Yorkshiremen), and fields that had become a mere chaos of shell-holes: and now for the first time experienced heavy shell-fire. I vaguely remember that the chief trench was called Quadrangle; that there was another named Pearl Alley, and that our 9th Battalion headquarters were in a deep dugout in a copse, possibly the one called Bottom Copse, but that first day amid the then unfamiliar scenes of slaughter and destruction, pervaded by the equally unfamiliar " battlefield smell " of churned up earth and rotting corpses, was dream-like in quality, and left but a hazy memory.

Orders came for the Brigade to move on the night of the 13th/14th July to a position in front of Mametz Wood, and from there to attack Bazentin Wood. On the 13th I walked over to Mametz Wood to see General Rawlins, who commanded the 62nd Brigade, and was in a German dugout on the western edge of the wood, which was to be our headquarters also. The wood was everywhere smashed by shell-fire and littered with dead—a German sniper hung over a branch horribly resembling a scarecrow, but half the trees had had their branches shot away, leaving fantastic jagged stumps like a Dulac picture of some goblin forest. It was the type of all woods blasted by really heavy shellfire, Bazentin, Delville, and the even more uncanny woods one knew east of Ypres in the autumn of 1917. Along the west edge ran a trench, from the side of which in places protruded the arms and legs of carelessly buried men, and as our men moved up that night to attack dozens of them shook hands with these ghastly relics. All the old " rides " through the wood were blocked by fallen trees and great shell-holes, and over all hung the overwhelming smell of corpses, turned-up earth, and lachrymatory gas. The sinister aspect of the wood was intensified that night by the incessant whistling and crashing of shells and the rattle of machine guns and illuminated by the German flares, Very lights, and the flash of bursting shrapnel.

Before dawn the 6th and 7th Battalions had carried the German front line—a trench running between the two woods—and Bazentin Wood beyond that, while owing to their right flank being exposed, they cleared also the village of Bazentin-le-Petit, (though not in their area), but the cost was appalling. Coöperation between artillery and infantry was then in its infancy, the " creeping barrage " not yet being developed, and it was hard for the infantry to keep up with their own barrage or alternatively to avoid walking into it. Seven machine guns were captured in the trench alone, but only after they had done deadly work, especially on the 7th Battalion, which lost fourteen officers killed. The enemy were not wholly cleared from the wood, and incessant appeals came back for bombs and smallarms ammunition, which were taken forward by parties of the 9th Battalion, under the Brigade bombing officer. During my second visit to the line that day, in company with General Hessey, we had just found Colonel Haigh of the 9th Battalion in a trench known as Forest Trench, when that particular trench became the object of a heavy bombardment as part of an abortive enemy counter-attack on the troops on our right, and for an hour we crouched in what remained of the trench while a stream of shells came roaring or screaming straight at us. When the shelling weakened the Brigadier walked along the trench ordering a general move-forward to occupy the north side of the wood, and from an orchard near Bazentin village we saw the enemy waves running back. Passing along to the west side, and just as we reached a light railway, we ran into heavy rifle fire from a German " pocket " left behind in the north-west corner of the wood, which subsequently cost us a good many casualties.

The following day as the result of an unfortunate misunderstanding the Brigade were ordered to withdraw, though, in fact, there was no one at hand yet to relieve them. The wearied troops streamed back, leaving only a company of the 1st East Yorks, belonging to the 64th Brigade, who had come up to reinforce our line. I was standing in Mametz Wood, when the Brigade Major called to me to collect everyone in sight, and take them to the front line, while he himself seizing a horse from a gunner rode round sending back the battalions. I got together about eighty men, and joined them on to the returning battalions, then wandering round Bazentin Wood found the Brigadier sitting in a shell-hole, meditating gloomily over the risk which had been incurred. He gave me a note for General Headlam, commanding the 64th Brigade, who we understood to have his headquarters in Bazentin village on our right. On reaching the village I found it empty and being heavily shelled, so after trying the cellars turned south and eventually found General Headlam in a shell-hole. Villages made easy locations on the map, and were usually death-traps; for the former reason they were often laid down in orders as headquarters for brigades or battalions, and for the latter reason as often the headquarters found shell-holes in the neighbourhood to be more congenial. From the point of view, however, of the solitary liaison officer, the game of hide and seek under shell-fire had its drawbacks.

I rejoined General Hessey on the west side of Bazentin Wood, and spent that night there with the 7th Battalion. The following morning we established a fixed headquarters in a German dugout, the entrance to which had to be cleared first of a heap of corpses, but that same night the Brigade was relieved and marched back by way of Fricourt Wood to the back areas.

It had been a gruelling experience for the Brigade, which had lost 2,000 casualties out of about 3,300 effectives. A very large proportion of the casualties were fatal, particularly among the officers, and of my own old battalion most of those I had known best had been killed or badly wounded. Of the others, I grieved particularly over Colonel Mignon of the 8th Battalion, one of the most charming of the many fine men I knew through the War, who was killed while leading a bombing party like a subaltern, and I remember vividly seeing him lying on his back still clutching a rifle. In the later stages of the War commanders of brigades and battalions were constantly being enjoined to stay at their headquarters while a battle was in progress, and to make full use of attached officers in my own position, which has sometimes given rise to malicious criticisms among those who only came out in the later stages, but during the early Somme battles colonels and brigadiers were, as far as my experience goes, seldom to be found in dugouts.

The most startling experience of this first battle, apart from the carnage, was the total breakdown of communications. It came to be accepted as a general rule that in battles all touch with units, whether in one's own line or on the flanks, had to be personal, and though runners could carry messages, reliable information could only be obtained by personal contact with the officers in the different areas. This was the primary reason for the attachment to all

Brigade and Battalion headquarters of " Intelligence Officers ", though in normal trench warfare we were expected to make ourselves useful in a variety of other ways, especially in organizing a systematic service of observation, sniping, and provision of up-to-date maps.

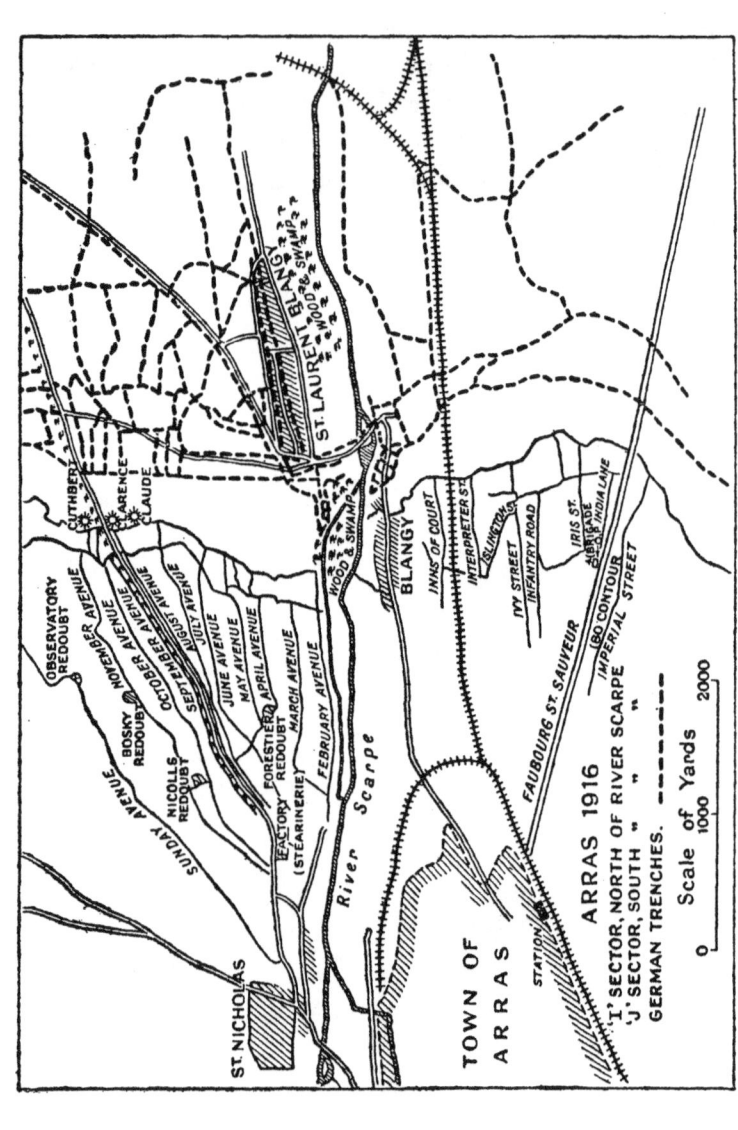

CHAPTER III

ARRAS—1916

WE journeyed north again via Hangest, where the landlady of an inn we had visited on the way down cried on learning that an officer of my old Battalion was among the dead, and before the end of July we had taken over a sector of trenches in the north-eastern suburbs of Arras, immediately north of the River Scarpe, known as "I" sector. The 21st Division held what were known as the H, I, and J sectors, our Brigade being responsible for the middle sector. On our left lay the 64th Brigade holding Roclincourt and Ecurie, on our right the 62nd Brigade, who held the eastern suburbs of Arras (south of the River Scarpe), known as the "Faubourg Saint Sauveur". Here were nearly intact streets running east of the railway straight into the German lines, but cut across by trenches and blocked by barricades. The houses here commanded an enfilade view of the German trenches opposite the 110th Brigade, especially the village of Saint Laurent Blangy, and in one of these houses I established my Brigade observation post. I attach a copy of a rough trench map I made at the time for my own use.

The strange coexistence of peace and war in this sector, combined with lovely weather, invested this period with an odd glamour of romance for at least one cog in the war machine. Our headquarters were in a great brewery in the Place Ste Croix—where we slept in fourposter beds—and my way to the trenches—which I often toured twice daily—lay along silent cobbled streets to the Pont St. Nicolas over the Scarpe, and thence from the " Stéarinerie " (a candle factory), along communication trenches cut in the chalk and paved with iron trays from the factory. The banks of the communication and support trenches were overgrown with tall rank grasses and wild flowers, and here and there were old shallow French assembly trenches, dating from the offensives of 1915, where one sometimes found pathetic French skeletons amid weeds two or three feet high. The trenches were not often shelled, and the general holiday atmosphere was only disturbed by occasional bursts of trench-mortar fire on the front line and, at four in the afternoon, with comic regularity, by a few shells on Arras cathedral. We were usually having tea at that time on the second floor of our brewery, and the shells flew straight overhead to the cathedral a few hundred yards away, but we had complete confidence that the efficiency of the German artillery would prevent any shells falling short and hitting our headquarters by mistake.

Just south of the Scarpe lay a wooded swamp, where one could stroll about within a hundred yards of the German sentries. There was a delightful summer-house usually surrounded by crowds of wildfowl, whose taste for this locality seemed undiminished by their casualties at the hands of General Rawlins, of the 62nd Brigade, who used to shoot them within a few hundred yards of the German line. The foremost post here was connected with our Brigade on the north side by a wire with bells, and an officer representing the 6th Corps supervised the river and intercepted floating messages with nets. He was, however, rewarded only by frivolous messages from English soldiers, I suppose addressed to " dear Jerry " and the like. At another point in this 62nd Brigade sector lay an isolated house, about four hundred yards behind the front line, but accessible over the top in daylight through long grass and stumpy trees. The cellars and lower story were full of Spanish furniture, bound in gold leather, and heaps of bric-à-brac littered the floor. I visited it with the 62nd Brigade Intelligence Officer the Sunday before we left Arras and noted a very fine enamel Christ on a large wooden cross.

Though there were very few civilians in Arras I found some refugees from St. Laurent Blangy, who gave me useful information about the cellars there, which I embodied with our own intelligence on a large map which gave me great pleasure. Our machine-gun company commander also had his headquarters in the town, in a fine house which had belonged, I think, to an architect, and where I often joined him and his transport officer (who came up every day, as did the regimental transport officers, from the horse-lines west of Arras) in convivial dinner parties. Once the transport officer—a cheery sportsman from Cork—drove me back through the pitch-dark streets at a furious pace, and in the excitement of the moment charged me over a heap of debris at one end of the ruined cathedral, and subsequently would remind me of the incident (which in some miraculous manner had left us and the horse intact) with the query " Do you mind the day we drove over Arras cathedral ? "

It was a very hot August, and an average walk of twenty miles a day in steel helmet and box respirator, with the glaring chalk reflecting the heat, could be very fatiguing, but the general glamour of this picturesque interlude made these peregrinations a labour of love. Moreover, it was not all walking— the Company and Battalion headquarters were usually in the old-fashioned type of dugout with doors and windows opening on the trenches, and a few feet of cover overhead, stores were plentiful, and there was a general atmosphere of cheerfulness. Especially do I remember—with a slight watering of the mouth after all these years—an 8th Battalion mess graced by the radiant presence of Dixie Smith, whose whereabouts could usually be divined when one heard a gramophone grinding out " Let the great big world keep turning ".

Unfortunately, the note of tragedy, ever close in war, was not wholly wanting to mar these idyllic scenes. In our front line were three mine craters, known as " Cuthbert ", " Clarence " and " Claude ", and mining operations mainly of a precautionary kind were being conducted by some New Zealand miners with the help of pioneers from our Division (14th Northumberland Fusiliers). One night the enemy blew a " camouflet " on the edge of the centre crater burying some miners and fourteen pioneers. At five in the morning I was at the spot with the Brigadier, who asked a miner if there was any hope of recovering any of the men alive, and I remember the miner—hands in pockets, a cigarette in his mouth, mumbling " Naw, flat as winkles ! ". The Brigadier rebuked a man who was not wearing a steel helmet, but it turned out that he had lost his helmet in the fall of earth under which he had lain for five hours.

This peaceful period was also interrupted by a raid carried out by our 8th Battalion. An officer of the Intelligence Corps—I think it was Tuohy, who later wrote a book about the work of his service—came down to us that night in the hope of interrogating a prisoner, but no prisoners were taken ; in fact no Germans were seen. Warned presumably by our preliminary bombardment, they had apparently vacated their trench. This was very unfair on their part, especially as our bombardment had cost £10,000, and we badly needed an identification, but as a distinguished Socialist politician once said to me, " What makes internationalism so hard is the absence of the British spirit abroad ". One of the most vivid incidents in the grimly realistic play " Journey's End " is the insistence on an impossible raid, an incident which must have struck a responsive chord of memory in every ex-infantryman.

I watched the preparation of many raids and never wavered from the conviction that the sole chance of success lay in surprise attacks, carefully prepared on a foundation of definite knowledge of the ground and the enemy's dispositions. Later, in the Hohenzollern Redoubt Sector, the Brigade carried out a raid on these lines with complete success. I think everyone in the line realized this, but to the end corps commanders persisted in ordering raids regardless of local conditions and with an arbitrary time-limit—often twenty-four hours' notice—and usually with the condition of a great artillery programme. What commonly occurred was that the enemy finding his wire being ostentatiously shot to pieces, withdrew his posts to the flanks of the threatened trench : and when the forward troops (by means of an admirable system of light signals, much superior to our own) gave warning, down came a barrage of shells, trench-mortar bombs, and enfilade machine-gun fire on the gaps in the wire and the jumping-off points of the raiders.

The Germans themselves raided us much less frequently, but when they did so it was an unpleasant experience. Their favourite method was to cut the necessary gaps in the wire, and simultaneously isolate and stupefy our posts, by a very short, but terrific and accurate trench-mortar bombardment, and on one such occasion our 62nd Brigade lost twenty men before anyone realized what had happened, nor was there anyone left to tell the tale. The German trench-mortar batteries were remarkably effective, both as to handling and equipment. If, as I used to believe, they always kept the lead of us in this respect, it was not due to any lack of spirit in our personnel. Once when going round the line before Monchy, in 1915 or 1916, with the Brigadier we noticed one of our trench-mortar bombs exploding short almost within our line, and on making enquiries found that the bomb having fallen on the parapet of the gunpit, the corporal in charge had reloaded it and fired it again—though he knew it was a matter of seconds before it should burst—and it burst about twenty yards away. It was the kind of action that in any previous war would have won the V.C.; thanks to the Brigadier's chance acquaintance with the circumstances, the corporal received the Military Medal.

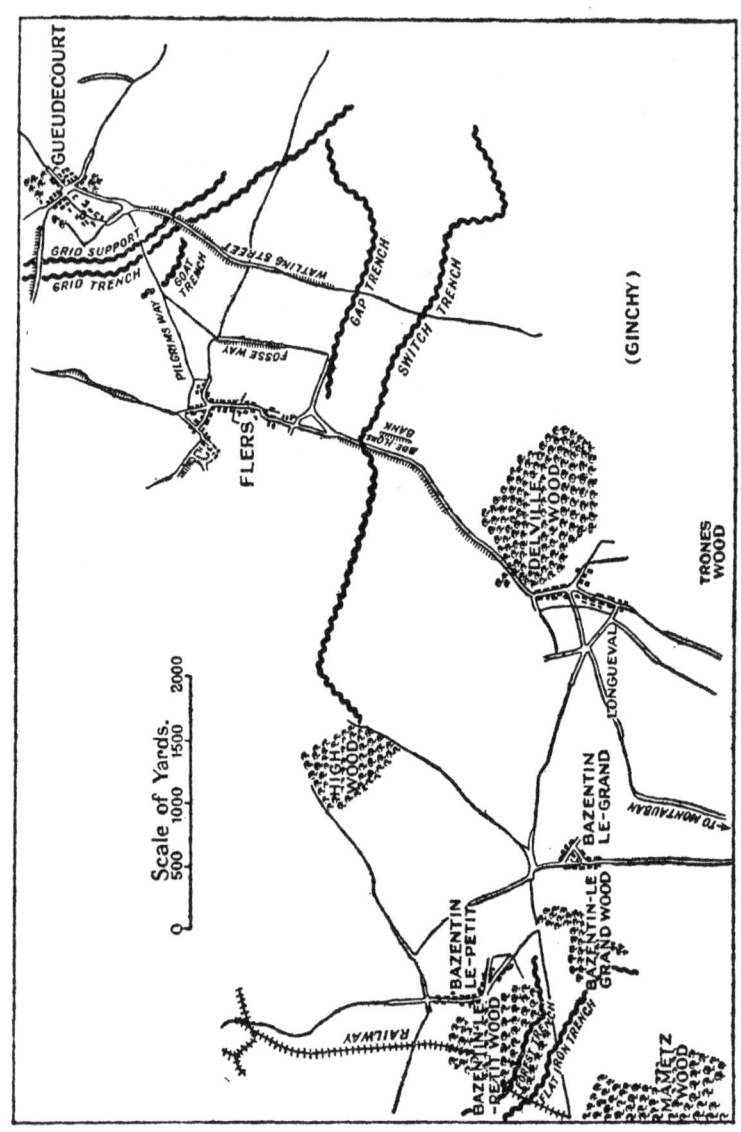

CHAPTER IV

THE SOMME ONCE MORE

Towards the end of August, 1916, the 21st Division was relieved by the 40th, who, I think were known as the " Bantams ", and withdrew to Liencourt, west of Arras, and from thence after a fortnight's rest entrained south again for the Somme.

We encamped on a great ridge south of the Albert-Fricourt road, wrongly called Fricourt Camp as it was several miles from Fricourt, and on the afternoon of the 19th September I rode with some Battalion representatives to Montauban village to reconnoitre the area between Montauban and Delville Wood. That night, the main roads being closed to infantry traffic, the Brigade marched across a deserted plain following my lead (as I had taken compass bearings during our afternoon ride), and I was terrified of going astray in the pitchy darkness. We arrived nevertheless at Montauban—which was packed with heavy artillery—and occupied the trenches we had reconnoitred in the afternoon.

About the 21st I walked up through Delville Wood in a drenching rain-storm (which did not improve the appearance of that dismal spot, smashed by shell-fire and littered with dead) to the remains of the village of Flers. My chief object was to find a suitable site for Brigade headquarters to occupy after the imminent attack on Gueudecourt village, which was to be our share of a more general offensive on the 25th. I found a bank running roughly north to south, close to the Montauban-Longueval-Flers road, and a few hundred yards from the heap of bricks which had been Flers. Nearby lay a disabled tank—for all I know the very tank which had just before walked into Flers village, thus making the début of the tank in modern war—and the site was marked on the map as " S.6 d 8.2 ". It was close to our existing front line, and a working party was soon busy digging a hole in the bank for our accommodation.

Somewhere in front of Delville Wood, at this time, I noticed a youth sitting bolt upright on the edge of a shell-hole, apparently studying his right hand which was half-raised. Getting no answer when I called to know what he was doing there, I approached him, and found he had evidently been dead some hours. It was the only case of the kind I ever came across and seemed horribly unnatural.

On the night of the 24th the Brigade moved up to a ridge, at one corner of which lay the new headquarters, while from its crest one commanded a view of Flers on the left, Gueudicourt village lying right in front, and Lesbœufs and Morval on the right. At 12.35 in the afternoon of the 25th—the unusual hour fixed for the attack—I was in the so-called " Switch trench" running along the crest of this ridge. I still have a German map on the back of which I made a rough panoramic drawing of the view while waiting for "zero". Straight in front lay the remains of Gueudicourt—a cluster of broken trees with the debris of the church in the centre, a road with two solitary trees leading from our ridge to the left edge of this village. To the left lay the ruins of Flers, to the right Lesbœufs, with a gaunt broken tower in the centre. Away beyond these three the skyline was broken, from left to right, by a line of poplars, the relatively extensive ruins of Bapaume, then Riencourt and Beaulencourt, and finally halfway between Lesbœufs and the skyline, the trees of Le Transloy.

Within a second or two our artillery barrage had burst out all along the line, the sound reminding me by some curious trick of memory of a mounted troop blazing away with revolvers at a circus I had once attended at Moscow. At the signal the 8th and 9th Leicesters rose out of their assembly trenches just below the crest I was on, and began walking steadily forward behind our bursting shells, while away to the right for miles one saw the irregular waves of our infantry, including, I think, the Guards Division. It was a fine and clear afternoon, and for a moment one could fancy oneself to be watching a field-day. The illusion did not last long, for within two or three minutes after the opening of our artillery the enemy counter-barrage began to fall—line upon line of black earth spouts from fifteen to twenty yards apart. Gueudicourt, Lesbœufs and Morval quickly disappeared in clouds of smoke and dust, and our own waves were soon swallowed in the torn brown landscape, for all this ground was already a wilderness of shell-holes.

No news came back, and at 4 o'clock I set off with two orderlies to find out how matters stood. Avoiding the village of Flers, which was literally hidden in a cloud of red brick-dust raised by a stream of heavy shells, I worked across country to the German front line before Gueudicourt, and walked along it from west to east. Here and there were small knots of men, and one or two wounded officers, who, as was not unusual in such cases, fancied they were the only survivors and could give no definite information. Bullets were whizzing round, and after a while it became clear that there was a large gap on our right in this trench, while the trench between this one and Gueudicourt village was actually being shared between our men and the only partially-expelled German garrison who were sniping actively in all directions. At the gap on our right—where a hasty block had been made—I found Captain Tooth, Adjutant of the 9th Battalion, who greeted me with the words, " Thank God, here you are ". I discovered later this address was not so flattering as it sounded; it was due to the fact that I was " wearing wash-leather gloves and carrying a malacca cane as though in Piccadilly ", and consequently conveyed the impression that things must after all be normal. He informed me that his

Colonel was wounded, and in a dugout in a sunken road leading to the second trench that was being shared with Germans. Leaving him I found Major Beardsley, second-in-command of the 8th Leicesters, and together we made a dash across the open to the Colonel's dugout. Though the distance was short, Beardsley's orderly was hit by a sniper on the way, and I learned then that every orderly who had been sent back with messages to Brigade headquarters had been knocked out on the way. One of my own two was also, as I found out subsequently, wounded on his way back with a note I had given him. After getting the necessary explanations from the Colonel as to the whole situation, I made my way back to Brigade headquarters, returning safely by about 7 o'clock. I remember the German trenches were littered with hairy knapsacks and cigars lying beside the slits or "cubby-holes", in which the late owners had crouched under our barrage.

That night the 6th Battalion moved up to the western edge of the still-untaken village of Gueudicourt, and as patrols found it was no longer held it was occupied the next morning. Early that same morning a tank moved along the partly German trench which had given so much trouble, and enabled our men to clear it, taking numerous prisoners. The Brigade had by now taken all their objectives—as they had done at Bazentin in July—and the casualties were I think about 1,400. Unfortunately our casualties did not end with the collapse of the enemy's resistance.

Colonel Drysdale, a very fine officer, who had only just rejoined the Brigade to command the 7th Battalion, was killed by a sniper on the 27th while being shown the line in which his Battalion was relieving the 6th, and my friend George Gillett, of the 6th Leicesters at whose invitation I had originally joined that Battalion in 1914, was killed by a stray shell while sitting in a trench, at the very moment when the Commanding Officer, Colonel Challoner, had told his servant to go up and fetch him down into the dugout for tea. We had been privates together in the autumn of 1914, and Gillett, receiving an invitation from Colonel Challoner to join him as an officer and bring a friend, gave me the offer. Not very long before the battle of Gueudicourt—while the Brigade was resting—Gillett and I went on leave together and lunched with members of my family on his way through London. On our return to duty he confided to me that he was very depressed, and had left England with a feeling of certainty that he would never return. His melancholy on this occasion had impressed me as he was blessed with a strong sense of humour. I remember a peculiarly grey winter's day at Berles when the Brigadier and I were wading through the mud in his company's sector, under heavy rain, and Gillett remarked aside to me, " What a shame to bring you out on a day like this ".

On the evening of the 26th I was accompanied by the Divisional G.S.O. 3 on a tour to locate the position of our line. We found the village of Gueudicourt had been left empty by our men—prudently enough, as a continuous series of small shells were screaming over our heads into it—and that they had dug in all round on the outside, except for a gap of some hundreds of yards on the left. A man we had asked to guide us led us through the gap and nearly into the enemy lines, and we encountered at this point some twenty horses standing in Nomansland—the legacy of a cavalry reconnaissance inspired by some pathetic wave of optimism. We were probably never at any time in the Somme campaign within measurable distance of a break-through, but one understood the temptation to find a use for our magnificent cavalry, whose individual members always impressed me by their efficiency and intelligence when one came in contact with them, mostly, of course, on dismounted work. We eventually found Colonel Challoner seated on the ground talking paternally to a somewhat dejected circle of men, while the field-gun shells whizzed overhead and banged down a hundred yards behind. He took us round the line and gave us all the information we wanted. Two or three days later the Brigade was relieved, and while the relief was in progress Colonel Unwin who had succeeded Colonel Mignon in command of the 8th Battalion was wounded by a shell at a congested spot on the road. He was an expert on shells, having a taste for collecting fragments and "nosecaps", and was said to have remarked "fancy being knocked out by a wretched whizzbang!".

CHAPTER V

MUD : THE HOHENZOLLERN REDOUBT IN 1916

THE Brigade entrained north to Saillaux, and from thence marched about twelve miles to our old friend Hangest, from whence it marched back again to somewhere close to Saillaux and entrained again, rather in the manner of the Duke of York, " who marched them up to the top of a hill and marched them down again ". During this humorous proceeding a staff officer drove, with a senior staff officer, in the latter's car to Amiens, to buy vessels for drawing water in order that the men might get water at the station, but did not arrive till the Brigade had gone as the officer who owned the car had taken too long over lunch. I mention the incident not as typical—I don't think it was—but as a warning to any future staff officer, should such chance to read this, that incidents of the kind get noticed and attract unfavourable comment.

We went north by way of Pont-Remy, and early in October took over the famous Hohenzollern sector, south of the La Bassée Canal, from which we were divided by the Cambrin and Guinchy sectors.

Hohenzollern Redoubt shewing Fosse and Slag-heap
Craters indicate Right Boundary of 110th Brigade

MUD: THE HOHENZOLLERN REDOUBT

The most novel feature for us of this sector was an uninterrupted series of mine craters stretching right along the front line and making an attack or even at most places a large raid, impossible for either side. Our Brigade headquarters were in shelters off one of the main communication trenches (Hulluch Alley), and henceforth we all lived continually in trenches. Behind us lay the ruined village of Vermelles, occasionally swept by enemy machine-gun fire and to the right lay the old Loos battlefield. The second main feature of this line was the enemy's highly organized system of trench-mortar bombardment. This was greatly facilitated by his possession of a colossal slag-heap—it was a mining district—called Fosse 8, which in that flat, devastated country dominated the local situation. It was full of observation posts from which the trench-mortar fire was controlled, especially that of a battery of heavy trench mortars tucked away in deep emplacements (as revealed by aeroplane photographs) immediately behind the slag-heap and therefore untouchable. These mortars, especially the hated "rum-jar" or medium type, were a curse in our forward area, and being ourselves weak in that arm (except for the light Stokes mortar) we attempted various schemes of artillery retaliation without much effect. One could usually see these unpleasant objects in mid-air, and gauge more or less accurately where they would fall, but if one happened to be waist-deep in mud the prevision was not much use. However, the subterranean burrowings of our mining company suggested the idea of opening up a complete system of galleries and dugouts for the garrison of the forward area, with shafts running up to all the posts in the craters which constituted Nomansland, and when we left the sector in February, 1917, the trenches were virtually disused. This resulted in a great saving of life, but a decline in morale owing to the continuous underground life in the crowded unventilated tunnels.

I spent the month of November with the neighbouring 64th Brigade, acting as their Brigade Major in the absence on leave of the real one, being attached for that month as a "staff learner". Though this Brigade were in the line on our left holding the Cambrin sector their headquarters were in a house in the only partly destroyed mining village of Annequin, and at the entrance to one of the communication trenches there actually sat an old lady selling apples and, I think, newspapers. The sector was very quiet, the weather fine though cold, and the change from the stuffy underground life of my own Brigade's sector was delightful. I retain consequently a most pleasant memory of my stay, which gave me the same curious kind of enjoyment as our period in front of Arras.

At that time I had not yet become an expert in the interpretation of aerial photographs and when on one occasion an artillery Brigadier called at the Brigade headquarters, and asked for suggestions as

MUD: THE HOHENZOLLERN REDOUBT

to targets, I showed him some photographs I had not studied and indicated some obvious centres of activity, tracks and works suggesting battery positions, headquarters, etc. We identified these on the map and he departed in great good humour promising to " strafe them like blazes ": but after he had gone I found to my horror that the obvious targets I had shown him were all on our side of the line, as we had been looking at the photographs upside down! I left to General Headlam (commanding 64th Brigade) the task of explaining this to the gunner.

On another occasion a cadaverous-faced officer with the intense gaze of a fanatic called on me. He belonged to the Special Brigade of the R.E. which had been our answer—and an effective if belated answer—to the German use of gas. He came to get any local information about his special subject, but entertained me also with pleasant anecdotes about recent happenings elsewhere, especially of a recent gas bombardment of ours after which, he remarked in a sepulchral tone and with a ghastly smile, " the cold meat trains had been busy for three days ". The Special Brigade produced a cheerful little magazine called, I think *Chemical Warfare*, which never circulated further down than Brigade headquarters. Much of the material consisted of rather grisly details gathered from prisoners or refugees and statements from other sources regarding enemy casualties from our gas. Their chief was an Oxford don, who had become an officer in one of our battalions until, just before we left for France, the War Office suddenly remembered the offer of his services in his own special subject.

The 110th Brigade were relieved in December, and spent Christmas in Auchel, a mining town, where the men were most generously welcomed by the inhabitants. I spent most of the time in bed on account of a fall when mounting a horse (a beast who was being sent back as incorrigibly vicious, but which I undertook to ride in the "*chaleur communicative d'un banquet*" at a too hospitable mess), and was deeply impressed by the kindness and attention of my hosts, a watchmaker with miner sons and several daughters. I don't think any French civilians did as much for the troops as these mining families. I have always liked miners and found that our own—we had some hundreds of Midland miners in the Brigade—were in the first class for discipline, courage and intelligence, and I was always glad to have them as orderlies or observers. When at a later date my batman (a domestic servant *de carrière*) was wounded I took on in his place one of my coal-miner observers who adapted himself brilliantly to this novel *métier*.

In January, 1917, we returned to the Hohenzollern sector where we found the whole fabric of the trenches had been loosened by the alternate frosts and thaws. Much labour was entailed thereby, but despite constant efforts the communication trenches became neck-deep for short men, several of whom had narrow escapes from this horrible form of death. It was nevertheless during this period that the Brigade carried out an admirable raid, which succeeded completely, because it was the result of a careful study of the local conditions, adequate preparation, and the application of elementary psychology. Anticipating the orders from Corps headquarters for the execution of a raid, I set to work from the moment we returned to the trenches to examine every possibility, and was able to suggest in broad outline a scheme, which was already under preparation when the orders came and which was eventually carried out.

The objective chosen was a salient and isolated German post known as "Diamond Point". The miners opened shafts into Nomansland as near as we dared and at the critical moment the artillery and trench-mortars opened feint bombardments on other points in the German line and on the wire in front of these other points, together with a smoke barrage, the latter especially on the great slagheap, blinding the observers on its face and the trench-mortars behind it. The raiding parties—an awesome spectacle with their blackened faces—sallied out from the shafts and exploded "Bangalore torpedoes" in the wire, which had been deliberately left uncut. The torpedoes did not work with full effect, a fact which limited the success of the enterprise, but a sufficient gap was made, the German posts surrounded and rushed, and within a few minutes the raiders were back with eight prisoners. That the Germans were completely mystified was shown by the direction of the retaliatory fire, which fell on the sectors opposite those visited by our sham bombardment, and even on the trenches of the Brigade on our flank, and I was convinced from what I saw and heard that they did not discover what had really happened until daybreak. In this raid the elements of surprise and deception were fully exploited, and miners, engineers, artillery, infantry and intelligence work were all used together in coöperation, and it is worth dwelling on as a contrast to the sledgehammer methods so poignantly illustrated in " Journey's End ", and alas ! so usual throughout the War, both in small episodes and on the largest scale. Once when a German prisoner was being interrogated by the Divisional Intelligence officer I asked whether he preferred being in the line opposite ourselves or the French. The reply was to the effect that though the English fired a great deal more they were preferable to the French as with the English one at least knew what was going to happen !

The mention of prisoners reminds me that while we were in this sector two German prisoners of war who had escaped from, I think, Mazingarbe prisoners of war camp, fell into the arms of our foremost sentries through slipping on the mud of a crater and were captured in this way when within about twenty yards of their own front line. They had lain hidden by day and walked by night, finally walking over the top right through our trench system. In one village they passed through they were addressed by some Tommies, but one of them who spoke English replied, " No time, R.E.'s ! ", and the incurious Tommies took no further notice.

I could tell many anecdotes of this want of curiosity —often resulting in an ignorance of their own whereabouts and of the units round them which must have been the despair of German Intelligence officers when they were taken prisoners. A court-martial officer who visited us at Arras told me a story of a case then pending which concerned a soldier who after very distinguished service disappeared in the Ypres salient and was identified a year later living in a dugout close to the Ypres-Commines Canal, where he had been living ever since his disappearance, in company with numerous units which successively occupied the dugout, whose rations he shared. The curious thing was that none of these passing companions ever found his presence odd : they vaguely concluded he was " something to do with the R.E.", and accepted him as part of the incomprehensible machinery of war. This lack of inquisitiveness—and habit of taciturnity—certainly helped our army to keep secrets (which were given away in London, but not usually by the army in France) and to maintain its moral. There was never, among our fighting troops at least, even a semblance of the dangerous spirit of mutiny which (unknown to us) existed in some allied units in 1917.

CHAPTER VI

THE HINDENBURG LINE

IN February the Germans began their carefully prepared retreat to the famous Hindenburg line, and our Division was relieved in order to go south and join in the pursuit. The Brigade began to follow up from the old Pommiers-Berles area, which we had last seen in the summer of 1916. Only seven months had passed, but already our long winter there seemed prehistoric. I visited Monchy-au-Bois, the village which then had lain in the German lines, and examined the German headquarter dugouts, and the little cemetery where several English officers, including poor Champneys, lay buried, inspected three great concrete barriers across the Berles-Monchy road, and watched some French territorials burying the Frenchmen who had lain out so long in Nomansland on the same Berles-Monchy road. I remember riding round Adinfer Wood, from which German batteries had occasionally shelled us, trying in a blinding blizzard to find an alternative route for our infantry to march, the only available road being congested with artillery and transport. There was, however, no alternative route, and we eventually marched by

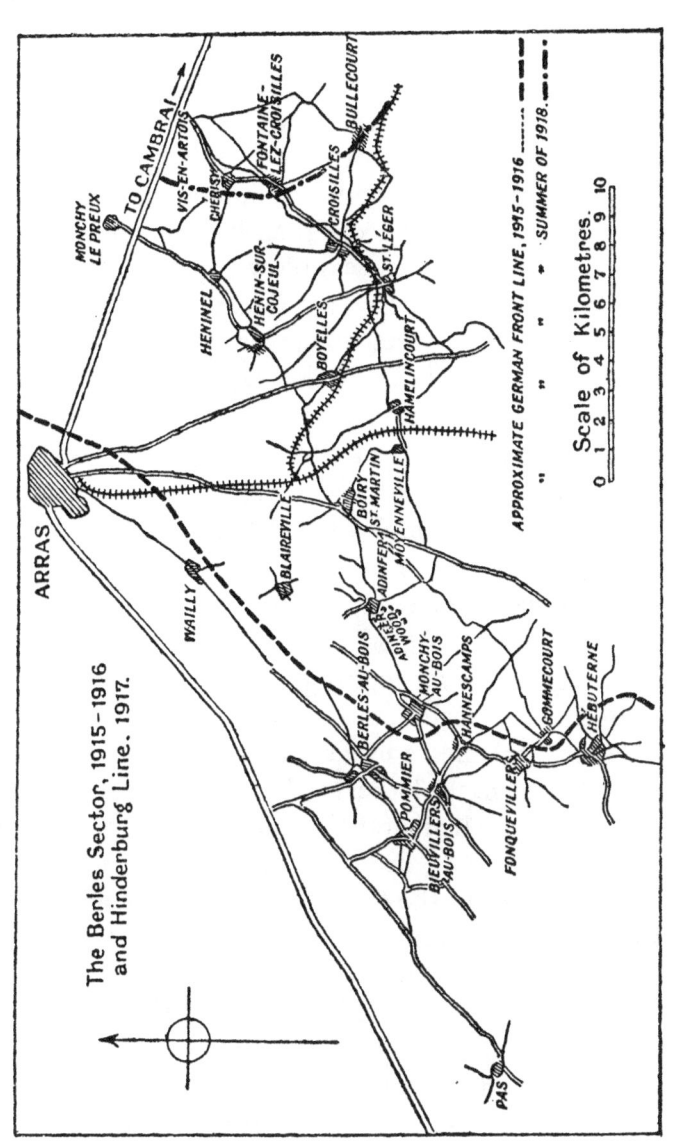

Adinfer village to Boiry St. Martin, the first village where we were able to observe the thorough destruction left by the Germans in their wake.

Right across the belt of land stretching back from the old trench-line to the new Hindenburg line it was the same story: every cross road had become a great mine-crater, every house was blown up so scientifically that the roofs encumbered the floors, and even cellars were hard to find, trees wherever possible had been systematically cut down, wells had been everywhere destroyed. As we advanced across this wilderness the horses had to be sent ever longer journeys to be watered, and as the weather was bitterly cold they died like flies. The mules stood the test far better.

From Boiry we moved by Hamelincourt and Moyenneville, completely destroyed villages, to St. Leger, where we found the British front line just east of a great railway cutting running from St. Leger to Boyelles. A neighbouring Division captured the village of Croisilles while a Brigade of our Division drove the enemy off the roads between Croisilles—St. Leger and Henin-sur-Cojeul. Our Brigade then moved forward and occupied this line, the village of Croisilles being in the front line. Two companies of the 7th Leicestershires, under Evans and Hemphill, occupied Croisilles, one company headquarters in a cellar at the south end of the village, the other in a sunken road on the north side. I remember a crucifix in the Northern Quarter standing significantly amid the debris, but we blew it up for fear it had been

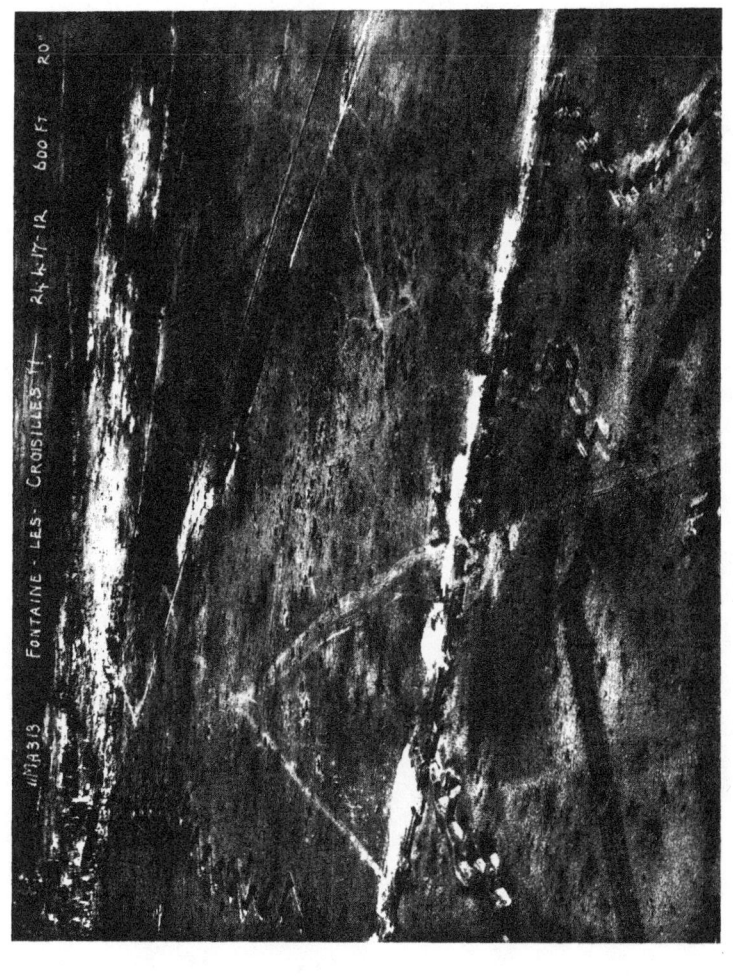

A "Close-up" of Hindenburg Support Line in Front of Fontaine Village Note the V-shaped Belts of Barbed Wire.

The Hindenburg Line at Fontaine-lez-Croisilles, April 1917, shewing V-shaped Belts of Barbed Wire. The Support Line ("Tunnel Trench") is the Left Hand Trench of the Two Parallel Trenches.

THE HINDENBURG LINE

left as a calibration point for the German artillery. A day or two earlier we had watched from afar the offensive on the Arras road on our left which gave us the dominating height of Monchy-le-Preux, and had watched too the rain of shells bursting on that height at a moment when, as we heard later, it was full of our unfortunate cavalry horses.

During the remainder of March and the first days of April the German outpost line was being gradually forced back on to the Hindenburg line, and by the middle of April the Brigade was holding what remained substantially throughout the summer the British line, despite many costly efforts to improve it. This line was really the front line of the Hindenburg system and lay about fifteen hundred yards east of Croisilles, crossing the dry Sensée brook. The trench, which became our front line, had been captured by other units, after a prolonged artillery preparation to cut the astounding network of barbed wire, many yards deep, which guarded it.

The Hindenburg line consisted of two great parallel trenches—of which we held one, as related above—each protected by dense masses of V-shaped wire entanglements, with lanes purposely arranged to be swept by concentrated machine-gune fire. The trenches were elaborately built with regular symmetrical traverses, numerous concrete " pillboxes " (generally known then, when we first encountered them, as " M.E.B.U.S." from the initial letters of the German words) and saps for machine-gun posts.

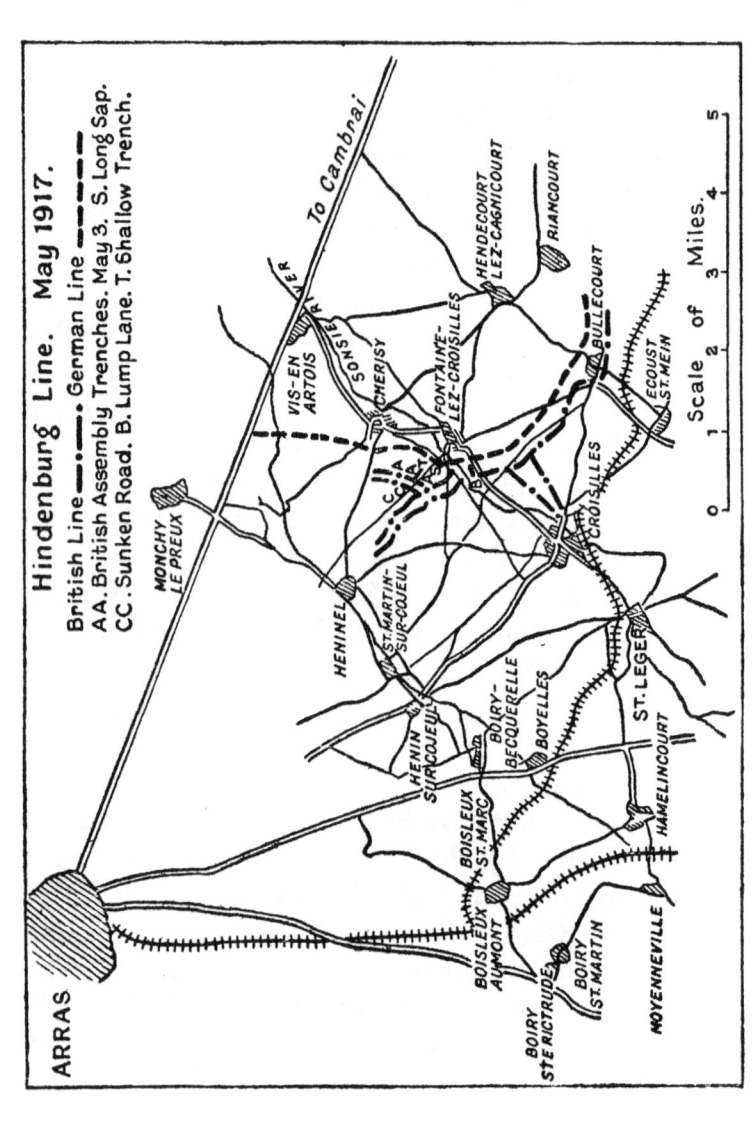

Fontaine Village and Hindenburg Support Line

The second line, which now became the German front line as far as our Brigade was concerned, was provided with a deep and continuous mined tunnel, running for miles underneath, and approached by shafts at regular intervals. The system embodied all the lessons of trench warfare learned since 1914, was a model of trench organisation, and fully justified its designers by the frightful casualties we incurred in trying to charge it—one might even say butt our heads against it—during 1917.

Though south of the Sensée brook only the front line was in our hands, the support or tunnel trench had also been taken north of the Sensée, on our left, so that at the end of April the German posts south of the Sensée, and opposite our Brigade, formed the apex of a triangle, their line here swinging back on a switch line running west of Fontaine—Cherisy—Vis-en-Artois. A scheme was therefore devised for turning the whole of the tunnel trench facing us, together with the original German front line on our right or south, which still remained in German hands, by a general attack from the north-west, and the 21st Division was detailed to coöperate in a great attack to be delivered on May 3rd from the north upon the switch line Fontaine—Cherisy—Vis-en-Artois.

Our Brigade was moved round (with a few days' rest in a camp near Boyelles) and on May 2nd we took over the sector facing Fontaine. The 64th Brigade were to attack down the tunnel trench southwards, our own to attack from the trenches marked A to A on the accompanying rough diagram. While walking round the new area before our Brigade took over its positions for the attack, I encountered one of my college contemporaries, Hine-Haycock, who was commanding a company of the K.O.Y.L.I. I spent half an hour with him discussing Magdalen days over burned rum; he explained to me he was on the point of leaving the Division to take on some staff job, I think, on Army Headquarters. I learned soon after that he was killed by a shell close to the spot where he had seen me off at the door of his dugout.

On one occasion during this preliminary tour, in order to gain better observation, I turned up one of the communication trenches (joining the tunnel trench with what had been for the Germans the front line), and found it literally heaped with British dead. The troops we were relieving had been clearing the recently captured tunnel trench, and had dumped all the corpses in this disused side trench. I also went out to the head of the long sap (marked S on the diagram), and discussed the ground in front of us—over which the attack was to be made next morning—with a corporal, who indicated a trench (marked T), which he said he had visited the previous night, and found it unoccupied and hardly more than a trace on the ground. Had his statement, which I duly included in my report, been believed, some lives would have been saved, as on the following day our 7th Battalion received orders to bomb-down this trench and merely

FONTAINE-LEZ-CROISILLES FROM NORTH-WEST SIDE ATTACKED ON MAY 3RD, 1917 exposed themselves to machine-gun fire in consequence.

That night our Brigade took over the new line. Several ammunition dumps were formed close to the assembly trenches but were accurately shelled by the enemy, and the Brigade bombing officer, Hinkley, who had recently returned from hospital after being wounded in Bazentin Wood, was again and more seriously wounded by a shell in the village of Heninel, while supervising the transfer of ammunition from the Brigade transport to the Battalion carrying-parties.

It must be borne in mind that from this time onwards the Brigade contained a constantly increasing proportion of officers and men who had already been wounded and had returned to duty, and of others who had been with it since 1915, and were feeling the strain in an increasing degree. The strain itself was, moreover, increasing absolutely: if our now lavish supplies of guns and ammunition enabled us to make constant attacks, so also did the Russian breakdown and other circumstances enable the Germans to reply with greater vigour. "Back areas" which had been regarded as normally quiet, i.e., areas from two to four or five thousand yards behind the front line, now constantly attracted the attention of the German artillery, while in areas still further back, likely points such as cross-roads, bridges and villages began to be troubled by the heavier artillery and high velocity shells, so that there was no longer any safety within a zone of four or five miles. Now began in particular the systematic development of counter-artillery work, i.e., the serious systematic effort by each side to put the enemy's artillery out of action, and the final result was that the trenches were, except when an attack was in question, often much quieter than the battery areas just behind. The steadily mounting casualties of the artillery personnel from the summer of 1917 onwards were eloquent proof of these changed conditions. Very few, however, of the hundreds I knew, and of those few hardly any in our own Brigade, ever complained or dwelt upon this. The average man continued to the end to tackle the work in hand at the moment in the traditional half-ironic, wholly philosophic, spirit of the British Army.

At midnight some new aeroplane photographs of the enemy positions reached Brigade headquarters and I took these up to the battalions about to attack. The 9th Battalion headquarters were in an unfinished dugout shaft, just beyond the sunken road, and in the forward assembly trench. Hundreds of men were sitting in the trench trying to sleep, in too many cases for the last time. As always the officers seemed glad to accept such encouragement about the general situation as I could give, while the old hands among the Tommies were sceptical yet quaintly cheerful, in a way characteristic of them.

The attack, which I believe was practically ignored in the English Press, was on the grand scale—on a front of ten Divisions, I think—and was a tragic failure. As far as we were concerned the reasons for this were clear. Delivered in pitch darkness, so that touch between units was rapidly lost, it was on too wide a front (several yards between each two men), and over too deep an area—one thousand yards of Nomansland had to be crossed before reaching the enemy. The ground had been imperfectly studied, so that several unexpected trenches were encountered in which many who had lost touch with their neighbours settled down. Finally, the enemy seemed well aware of our intentions, which had been discussed in detail over the telephone, no one realizing then that there were ways of " listening in ", and a heavy barrage came down simultaneously with our own. As usual, the German machine-gun fire was very effective. Nevertheless, some hundreds got right up to the enemy and kept up an isolated fight through the morning till they were rounded up by them or crawled back from shell-hole to shell-hole. One man I spoke to took four hours doing the thousand yards.

About 2 p.m. I was sent to see the headquarters of the two Brigades of the Division on our left flank, with whom we had just received orders to coöperate. I walked along the Hindenburg line, avoiding Heninel village which was being heavily shelled, and found both Brigade headquarters in a dugout north or northwest of that village. There I was informed that our rôle was to assist a fresh attack by this neighbouring

Division, by bombing down the trench marked T, which as mentioned above I had been told by a corporal was a mere trace. The Brigadiers, who were strangers to me, were not in a mood to encourage suggestions, so I hastened back to my headquarters, where I arrived with instructions about one hour before the attack was timed to begin.

Two of our companies started off to "bomb down" the supposed trench, and finding themselves merely exposed on open ground to heavy fire took shelter where they could, mostly in the sunken road nearby, and so spent the night. A complete withdrawal took place to our original line, and on the 5th the Brigade was relieved, having lost nearly a thousand casualties.

Soon after we returned to the old sector south of the Sensée brook, with Croisilles behind and Fontaine in front, holding as our front line the old Hindenburg front line as explained above. Brigade headquarters were now in shelters in the side of a sunken road running from St. Leger to Henin. About this time our Brigadier, General Hessey, went home sick and was replaced by Lord Loch, who as B.G.G.S. of the VIth Corps had planned the April battle before Arras. The preparations for that battle, involving the passage of two Divisions through the town of Arras and crowned, as was the case, with complete success, were described in a typed pamphlet which ought to be on the programme in the Staff College. It was a fascinating work.

It was about this time that I received the offer of appointment as a Flying Corps Intelligence Officer, the duties of this post being principally the study and distribution of the photographs taken in the air by the pilots or observers. Had I accepted this narrative would presumably come to an end at this point, as it would have involved settling down to a sedentary occupation in a permanent office.

The next few weeks were occupied with construction of trenches, wiring, and similar routine activities. We were much exercised about a curious sap, called Lump Lane, where our posts were in danger of being cut off by enemy raids which luckily did not take place, and I remember also some quarries with dugouts in them were bombarded with 12-inch shells, one of which (a " dud ") penetrated twenty-five feet of chalk and disappeared in the floor of the passage underneath. Company headquarters were mostly in " pill boxes ", which naturally having been built by the Germans to face the other way had their doors and thinner walls facing the enemy. We had the same experience later at Ypres, where there was often no other cover available.

On June 16th two battalions of the 62nd Brigade 12th and 13th Northumberland Fusiliers) were-ordered to pass up to out line and attack the tunnel trench soon after midnight. At about 8 p.m., so as not to be delayed by these battalions as they passed along our communication trenches, I went up to our front line to wait for the attack and report developments. There were in fact only two communication trenches (which we called " Nellie " and " Janet "), and both had to be used. Just as I reached our front line a heavy barrage descended on this restricted area through which I had come, and between 9 p.m. and midnight about four thousand shells fell around " Nellie " and " Janet ", showing that the enemy must have had exact information of our intentions, presumably from interception of telephone messages.

The effect on the incoming Battalions of having to struggle up to the line in the dark under heavy shell-fire can be imagined, and at zero hour our front line was in a state of chaos, all companies mixed up, Lewis guns lost and so on. The actual assembly trench was a newly-dug trench about twenty yards in front of our front line, and after the attack had begun I found in it dozens of bewildered men complaining that they had no orders. There was no result except that both Battalions sustained such heavy losses that they had to be amalgamated into one.

On our right, as already mentioned, the Germans still held the old Hindenburg front line, and a portion of this, extending from the rising ground called the " Hump " to Bullecourt, was attacked by troops on our right, I think London Territorials and the Naval Division, a day or two after the unfortunate episode just described. It must have been just before it that as we were dining in our cupola dugout a youthful-looking officer in an exceptionally dirty raincoat blew in. Taking him for a liaison officer of some kind the

THE HINDENBURG LINE

Brigadier invited him in an indifferent way to take a vacant seat at the end of the table and share a drink. We were all startled when after a few minutes our guest meekly observed that he was the Brigadier on our flank, and had come round in connection with an attack they were about to do. This was my only meeting with General Freyberg, V.C., one of the outstanding personalities of the War.

The attack was successful, but where the gap had existed between the British and German sectors of the trench there was for a time only a very shallow channel of communication, and anyone passing by daylight was under view by the Germans in the tunnel trench not many yards in front. Nevertheless, the G.S.O. 1 of a Division which was to relieve us, who had asked me to take him round our line, insisted on crossing this derelict gap in order to get a better view from the " Hump ", and our temerity was rewarded as I expected by half a dozen bullets from very close range. The incautious staff officer (who should of course have crawled) had, if I remember right, his helmet struck, and another bullet glancing off a pill box passed through my tunic and tie and scratched my chest. As I had to be inoculated I was duly posted as a casualty, and was presented with a wound-stripe to wear on my sleeve. This was rather absurd, but in fact not a few wound-stripes were put up for similar reasons.

Soon after this incident the Brigade was relieved and withdrew to a very wet camp near Blaireville and Wailly, where I rode in a tank for the first time, as there was a tank training ground and camp nearby. After a few weeks spent alternately in the old line and in rest in a camp at Moyenneville, the Brigade left the area and withdrew about the middle of August to Manin, a pleasant village west of Arras. This was the first time since February that those who had not been on leave had seen a civilian, and the first rest period of more than a fortnight's duration that we had had since December, 1916. Over seven months of almost continuous active service!

CHAPTER VII

THE BLOODY SALIENT (YPRES 1917)

THE most awful phase of the War for the British Army—the nightmare-like Flanders offensive of 1917—had now begun, and early in September the Division moved north to Caistre in French Flanders. From the train windows we watched at night the continuous line of lurid gun-flashes, and heard more audibly as we travelled north the steady growling which proclaimed the greatest artillery concentration the world has known. For a fortnight we waited uneasily, then moved up to one of the dismal camps of huts strewn over the Flanders back areas ("Scottish Wood" I think), and received orders to take over from an Australian Division the ground they were capturing north of the Ypres–Menin road, chiefly in the neighbourhood of Polygon Wood.

Time scatters the poppies of oblivion over most things, but the lapse of twelve years has not effaced the impressions of sordid horror and melancholy which this period of the War engraved on the mind. The general setting was inconceivably dreary and miserable, death or frightful mutilation by shell-fire were ever at hand to an unusual degree, and the effort

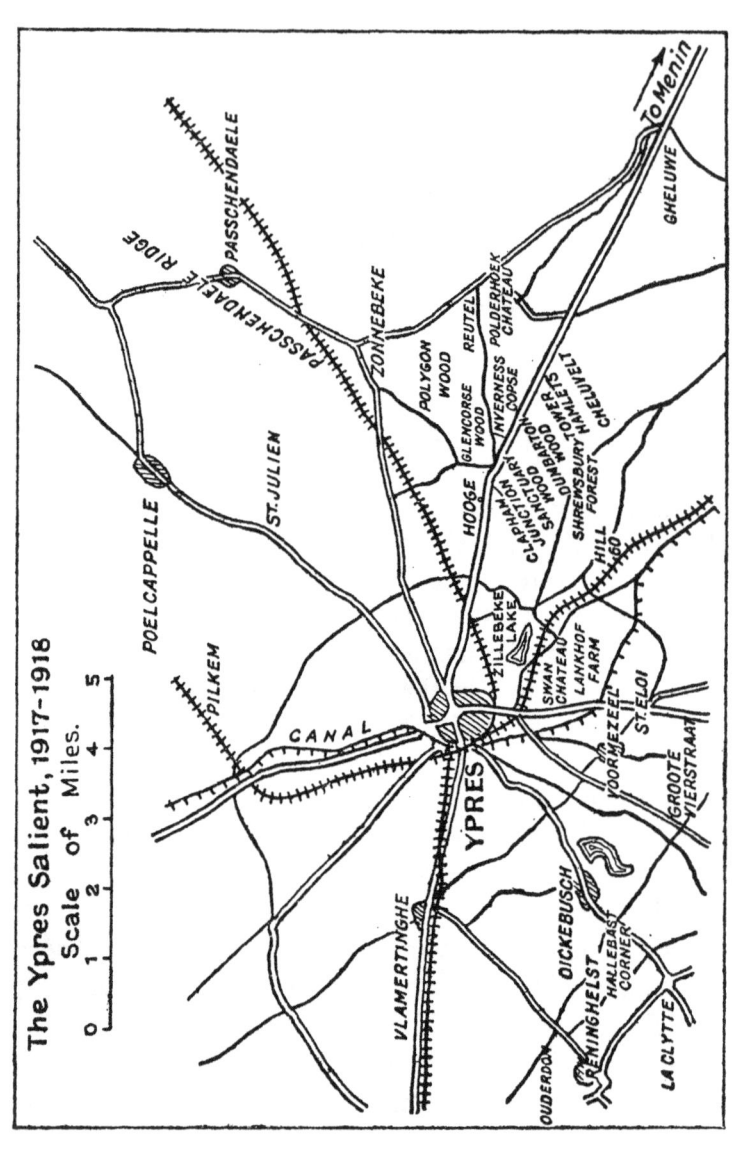

and sacrifice demanded of our Army—and willingly made—is scarcely credible. One hesitates to express oneself candidly for fear of being unfair to individuals untrained for such vast responsibilities, but when one compares the results with the dogged tenacity of infantry, gunners and transport men under loathsome nerve-wrecking conditions and the utterly prodigal expenditure of munitions and technical resources of every kind, one feels resentful of the doctrinaire fanaticism which kept the machine driving on at top-pressure, month after month, as though the gain of each few yards of water-logged craters was worth any sacrifice.

One felt at the time that the use of relief maps exaggerating the importance of contours, and the superstitious belief that every casualty we had was bound to be offset by at least one German equivalent, had fascinated General headquarters, and temporarily destroyed all sense of reality and proportion, creating a veritable madness for offensives. My vagabond life on the battlefields, which I had to explore pretty thoroughly, had made me marvel at the published dispatches which confidently stated that the enemy on the Somme suffered losses as great as our own, but my scepticism remained merely " agnostic " until I read in Mr. Winston Churchill's books the confirmation of my doubts. The " war of attrition " theory was a ghastly error, which in 1918 very nearly resulted in our destruction.

To understand the conditions in the Ypres salient

in the autumn of 1917 one must realize that this area had been on and off the most contested piece of the front since the winter of 1914. It had been the favoured scene for the enemy to try his experiments; this neighbourhood saw the first use of poison gas from cylinders, and later its renewed employment in the shape of "mustard-gas" shells, which in their first demonstration caused, we were told, as many casualties as the cylinder gas. The flat, dreary country, with its heavy rains, can never have been an earthly paradise, and the nearly three years' warfare had already made it a veritable "blasted heath", when we launched on July 31st the much-advertised offensive, heralded by an appalling bombardment with, roughly, a gun to every seven yards of front. Our shell-fire destroyed what remained of the old drainage system, and though the offensive of July 31st only very partially succeeded,* our line had been pushed on into the wilderness of shell-holes, which a rainy August soon filled with water. All roads and tracks except the Menin road had been totally obliterated, and the Army rapidly replaced them by plank roads for vehicles and "duckboard" tracks for foot transport. The enemy had concentrated every available gun and used ammunition with lavish prodigality, constantly smashing the new tracks which were as constantly repaired.

---

*Incidentally, the details of the initial plan of the attack at Ypres had been betrayed by a prisoner with a grievance, whose employment till shortly before had enabled him to become familiar with the scheme as a whole.

As the infantry line was pushed forward, each advance at great sacrifice, huge masses of artillery followed behind, the guns bunching together whereever a piece of relatively dry and unbroken ground could be found, and to the guns came, often twice a day, melancholy trains of pack mules and horses, their bodies caked with mud and loaded with ammunition, the weary drivers on foot urging them on amid shells crashing right and left, and shrapnel bursting overhead. Our massed guns—the crews often exposed without shelter day and night for several weeks—and wooden tracks—off which it was seldom possible to step on account of the condition of the ground—were visited at frequent intervals by bursts of shell-fire, always including a proportion of gas-shells. The " mustard " variety of gas-shell, already referred to, was difficult to distinguish from the more harmless kinds unless the stuff splashed one, when it caused severe blisters, but had two unpleasant characteristics —it lingered some hours and rose in vapour under the influence of the sun if there was any, and it contaminated clothes, so that persons thus affected could infect a whole dugout. The other types in fashion were lachrymatory (" green-cross "), chiefly intended to make the gunners wear masks, and the " blue cross ", which I think affected the heart and lungs, causing coughing and hoarseness.

It was into this inferno that on September 30th a party of officers from the Brigade came to reconnoitre Polygon Wood, and had a foretaste of the prevailing conditions, as nearly every member of the party suffered in some way from shell-fire. That night the relief of the Australians in the newly-captured Polygon Wood took place, the Brigade headquarters moving into Hooge crater dugout, a noisome hole under what had been Hooge Château, of which building not a stone could be found. The crater itself was an old one blown when the German front line had run there, at the side of the Ypres-Menin road, and alongside the site of the château. Besides accumulating a great mass of artillery, the Germans had concentrated all available reserves of troops—now greatly swollen by the Russian collapse—opposite us, and each gain we made was followed by heavy counter-attacks by fresh troops.

It was hardly therefore a surprise when early in the morning of the 1st October—just as our relief was complete—a great counter-attack was launched to recapture Polygon Wood. It was accompanied by the heaviest enemy shelling I had ever encountered—a series of barrages, distributed in depth over several miles of ground and maintained, with only occasional short lulls throughout the day. I got halfway up to the front line, but not having had definite orders to make contact, and knowing that whatever happened reinforcements could not get through such fire, I abandoned the attempt. My professional conscience was worried at the time, but it was really the sensible course.

The Brigade, as usual, stuck it out, and one

dramatic incident I give as I heard it from the Adjutant and a company commander of the Battalion concerned. Colonel Bent, V.C., of the 9th Battalion was in a " pill box " on the west side of the wood when a runner came in saying " S O S gone up from (the reserve) company ". " Then we'd better get on ", said the Colonel, and went forward with his headquarter personnel. Collecting the reserve company and everyone available, the Colonel led a counter-attack, and, struck down in the moment of victory, was last seen—for his body, doubtless blown to pieces, was not found—waving his pipe and calling, " Go on, Tigers ! " This very gallant officer was, I think only twenty-four at the time and was a civilian, but was so devoted to his work as a soldier that when granted ten days' leave he was back in less than a week with his Battalion.

Either that night or the next the Brigade was relieved by the 62nd Brigade, who were to take part in a grand assault on October 5th. Generally all the arrangements for reliefs were settled mutually by the Battalions concerned, but east of Ypres, just as east of Suez, " there weren't no ten commandments ", and I remember dropping guides at crucial points all over the routes of approach. While passing through Sanctuary Wood, which was full of field artillery invisible in the darkness, all the guns suddenly started an " S O S barrage ", which meant that one was in front of the muzzles of a dozen guns firing seven or eight rounds a minute. I encountered Colonel

Dicks of the 12/13th Northumberland Fusiliers, and accompanied him most of the way to the line in which he was to relieve one of our Battalions. He was a man with charming personality, with whom I had been on very good terms, but I never saw him again, as he was killed a day later in Polygon Wood.

We withdrew to Scottish Wood Camp, and I was instructed to attend on the morning of the fifth October at the headquarters of the 5th Divison as liaison officer for our own Division. The 5th Division were to attack on that morning, and were to call on our Brigade to reinforce in the event of a " breakthrough ". I arrived about five in the morning at the Divisional headquarters, a small street of very nice huts just outside the village of Dickebusch. It was a cold, dark morning, with drizzling rain and gusts of wind, and as standing on the plank-walk in front of the huts I watched the sudden illumination of the battle area by a line of gun-flashes and star shells, and heard the incessant rumbling of the guns, announcing that the attack had begun, I somehow felt the uncanny horror of the War even more than one would have nearer the scene.

The damp cold soon drove me into the warm and well-lighted " G " office, where I had about an hour in which to contemplate magnificent wall-maps, on which the arrangements for the attack looked astonishingly simple to execute. I think it was of this very attack that I obtained later the complete map of the artillery barrages, showing the successive 'lifts" exactly located on the map at every few minutes for over an hour. It seemed when one studied such a map by electric light in a dry and well-warmed hut, that such an attack could hardly fail, but if one stepped out into the cold and rainy blackness and thought of heavily laden men—carrying rations, rifle, entrenching tools, bombs, box-respirator—plodding forward round the squelchy edges of the water-logged shell-holes, under a rain of machine-gun bullets and bursting shells, the whole focus seemed to be altered. I was rescued from these gloomy thoughts by the appearance of a member of the staff, and I was kindly invited to breakfast in the " A " mess with the Divisional commander. Eventually, long after daylight, sufficient news had arrived by telephone from the Brigade headquarters concerned to make it clear that our Brigade would not be required that day to follow up a " breakthrough ", and I returned to my own headquarters.

During this battle a heap of red bricks known as Polderhoek Château—an outstanding feature, as even heaps of bricks were rare in that utterly razed area,—was taken and lost by our troops. It remained a thorn in the side of our Division, and subsequently resisted a number of " minor operations ". From time to time points of this kind became a sort of bogey: the moral factor is always intruding in war (as was also noticed by Napoleon).

Immediately afterwards our Brigade went again into the line, which as a result of the latest battle was

F

pushed forward to about fifteen hundred yards east of Polygon Wood, to include the Reutelbeck—on the map a stream, on the ground a huge lake owing to shell-fire—and the sites of Reutel and Molenaarelsthoek villages, which it would be quite inadequate to describe as merely blown to pieces: I remember going out with two of the Battalion commanders in a joint endeavour to identify Reutel, which had figured in a Divisional order as some kind of boundary mark, and that we could not agree as to the precise location! It was purely an exercise in map-reading, as not even one speck of brick-dust—let alone half a brick,—had survived.

An equally good illustration of the difficulties of this destroyed terrain was the case of the 7th Battalion headquarters. A guide provided by the Brigade we relieved, in order to take the Brigade Major and myself to this headquarters, having wisely disappeared, we spent several hours looking for it, as the map reference was about a thousand yards out, and as, owing to the whole area being under view from Polderhoek Château already referred to, there was no sign of life anywhere. We knew it was in one of the half-sunken concrete pill-boxes scattered among the shell-holes between Polygon Wood and the Menin Road, but there were dozens of these all under view. In the end we had to give it up and wait until a carrier-pigeon reached our dugout with the exact map-location.

During the next few days my time was spent either loafing in a corner of our stinking dugout at Hooge crater, or visiting our depressing line. The latter had become quiet enough in itself, but the routes to it were very frequently shelled. There were two routes, one south of Polygon Wood, past an old pill-box, called Black Watch Corner, the other north of the wood, and known as Jargon Track. This latter led through a deep hollow, always full of gas, from which nothing was visible but sky and shell-holes, and through a group of badly smashed pill-boxes—broken blocks of masonry with the steel rods sticking through the gaps—which enjoyed the sinister name of "Dead Mule Dugouts". The name was due to the presence of at least a dozen dead mules lying in heaps at the side of the track. There were a number of dead men as well. From this gloomy spot nothing but shell-holes could be seen, and the curious stale smell of gas, putrefaction and thrice disembowelled earth was overwhelming. One Battalion headquarters, I think the 8th, were in a dugout under the Butte de Polygone, a mound in the wood, and no mariner ever felt more relief on getting into port during a storm than one felt on one or two occasions in approaching that haven of refuge.

A remarkable feature of this period was the system of "Army barrages". Partly to deceive the enemy as to the precise time of our weekly attacks, partly to anticipate and break-up possible counter-attacks, the entire artillery on the Flanders Army front made a habit of firing massed barrages twice a day, usually before dawn and about twilight, for about forty minutes. In addition to these practice concentrations, the artillery were expected to fire rapidly for about twenty-five minutes whenever an " S O S " signal went up from the line, a frequent occurrence owing to the frayed nerves of the men in the line. In this way the average field-gun was supposed to fire about a thousand rounds a day, and as it took one mule or horse to carry up every six rounds, and the horse lines had to be many miles back, the strain on transport can be guessed. I have spoken already of the pathetic spectacle offered by the long strings of these weary mud-bedraggled animals plodding along the greasy shell-swept tracks. But in point of fact the volume of fire was greatly diminished by the enormous casualties among the gunners, which made it a sheer impossibility to serve many of the guns. There were cases when whole batteries were left derelict through the gradual extinction of the entire personnel. In addition, the ammunition dumps were constantly being set on fire by the ubiquitous enemy shell-fire, and not infrequently the whole area was illuminated at night by the lurid glare of burning dumps.

About the middle of October the Brigade was relieved and withdrew to Wardrecques. I went on leave and happened to be in London during a heavy air-raid one night. I was very cross at being awakened and asked to " listen to the barrage ", and composed myself to sleep again after remarking contemptuously, " Do you call *that* a barrage ? " Though it seems incredible now, I know I was acting quite naturally at the time, which shows how one can get accustomed to most things.

Returning about November 2nd I found the Brigade back in Polygon Wood, but everything much quieter as the centre of gravity had shifted further north to Passchendaele and Poelcapelle, where the authorities continued, as they doubtless expressed it, to " kill Germans " till the end of November. While I had been away Hooge crater dugout had been flooded owing to injudicious attempts to enlarge it, and General Rawlins, of the 62nd Brigade, had been killed by a shell at the very door of the dugout. He had gone out to supervise personally the unloading of some wagons which had been interrupted by a burst of shell-fire. The incident was characteristic of his disregard of danger, which he had shown among other ways by a habit in ordinary trench warfare of walking over the top instead of by the communication trenches as was laid down in orders for everyone else. At about the same time our Brigade transport lines were bombed by enemy aircraft, and all the riding horses except one, but including my own, were wounded. My horse, a very distinguished-looking Irish chestnut hunter, had eventually to go to hospital, and I never saw him again. I had bought him in England, and had brought him out with me to France as nominally the Brigadier's, not being entitled to have a horse myself.

After a fortnight we were relieved by a New Zealand brigade, and withdrew from this dismal area to somewhere west of Arras.

CHAPTER VIII

WAITING FOR THE MARCH OFFENSIVE

THE Division now received orders to proceed to Italy, and the Brigade had detailed instructions for the train-journey when an unexpected diversion occurred. The Cambrai offensive, executed on principles diametrically opposed to those followed at Ypres, had just taken place and had been attended by the success it deserved. Unfortunately the men who should have been guarding the flanks of our attack (to say nothing of exploiting the success) had perished uselessly in the Flanders mud, and the Germans in a brilliant counter-attack broke through on the exposed flank. Consequently our orders to proceed to Italy were cancelled, and the Division was rushed from the Chilers area to Tincourt, and from thence by road to the St. Emillie–Epehy front. Everything was in confusion: at Villers Faucon the Brigade waited for two hours in heavy rain for orders from the Brigadier and Brigade Major who had ridden on to the shattered Brigade we were to relieve, and our transport did not catch us up for several days. I remember the latter incident as I nearly froze at night in the absence of a blanket

The Epéhy Sector, Jan.-March 1918
Right Half of Sector.

or even a warm overcoat, which I, being on the Brigade headquarters, was in the bad habit of leaving our transport to carry when we were on the move.

The Lancashire Brigade we relieved had been holding a very long front, and had evidently not been anticipating an attack, for the enemy had penetrated to within two thousand yards of the Divisional headquarters capturing well-stocked canteens, officers' messes, battalion offices, and gum-boot stores. In the village of Villers-Guislain they even captured a number of heavy guns which had been pushed forward there to fire in enfilade to assist our Cambrai offensive, and somewhere near Vaucellette farm we found an artillery major lying dead in pink silk pyjamas, rifle in hand, in front of his battery headquarters, which he must have awakened to find in Nomansland. A Divisional headquarters at Heudicourt had abandoned quantities of personal belongings, such as field boots, clothes and maps; and much valuable equipment including electric lighting sets had been abandoned by field survey and other technical experts. A force of cavalry had been rushed forward as a stop-gap, and throughout our stay a large number of dead horses in Nomansland formed a landmark. The British Army had been so sedulously cultivating the offensive spirit since 1916 that the possibility of our being ourselves attacked had ceased to be reckoned with. By the end of the next summer the contrary tendency was naturally uppermost.

Happily the Germans could not press their advantage, and the Brigade settled down to dig hastily a new set of trenches east of Epehy village. I had to locate these trenches on the map as they were dug, which was rather complicated as the maps proved inaccurate in respect to various little copses and similar landmarks, so I had much amusement plotting them off new aeroplane photographs besides pacing them on the ground. Owing to the general lie of the ground the conditions were ideal for observation, and I had my observers in two posts, one shared with the artillery in the south end of Epehy village, the other in a detached house on the east side, where the R.E. made me a well-concealed concrete shelter with a ladder leading to an eyrie in the roof. Here my observers sat with a very powerful telescope lent by the VIIth Corps, and we never had more distant or extensive views over enemy country than here. Unfortunately, as will appear, full advantage was not taken of the evidence we collected. Before Christmas Lord Loch left us owing to illness, and was succeeded for a few months by General Cayley. I have spoken of Lord Loch's plans for the Arras offensive, and may add in regard to his service with the Brigade that he was easily the most brilliant staff officer I met during the War, with a highly developed gift of clear reasoning and lucid expression, and a genius for visualising and interpreting a map.

My chief memory of those months is of very early rising during a hard winter, for, as there were no

THE EPÉHY SECTOR, JAN.-MARCH 1918.
LEFT HALF OF SECTOR. (POPLAR TRENCH OUR FRONT LINE)

communication trenches until February (it being first necessary to build the system of fire trenches), I had to tour the trenches before daybreak. This meant starting about 4 a.m.—usually in sleet, heavy rain or a snowstorm—and being back by about 8 a.m.

In February I spent a week with the 48th Squadron R.A.F., studying the interpretation of aeroplane photographs. It was a squadron of " Bristol Fighters ", carrying an observer as well as pilot, and I was able to make my first flight while there. It was naturally very interesting to me to see the opposing trench systems from this novel angle, but I was rather relieved to land, after about an hour's flying, as an encounter with an enemy 'plane the first time one was up would have been alarming. The interpretation of aeroplane photographs is an art as well as a science, for considerable practice is needed to become really expert. A photograph was developed ready for inspection within twenty minutes of the pilot's return to the aerodrome, and if the various intermediary Intelligence officers and messengers were efficient copies were delivered to Brigades within twenty-four hours and to Battalions in the line in from twenty-eight to thirty hours.

Few people—even, I found, air pilots—realize into what an elaborate and fascinating science the interpretation of air photographs was developed. Circular objects, such as shell-holes, haystacks or bushy trees, which without shadows would appear from above as mere circles, appear on a photograph with individual characteristics, due to the shadows, as definite as when seen from the ground, although indistinguishable to the inexpert eye. In a photo of a normal trench sector, when conditions remained more or less stationary for many months, the practised eye could distinguish between used and disused trenches (by the depth, tracks on the ground near by, or signs of new work), machine-gun from trench-mortar emplacements, which, again, might be open or covered and for light or heavy guns : between trench tramways, light railways, cable trenches, air-lines, and tracks for man or beast. At times very careful examination was required to distinguish latrines and sump pits, or observation posts in trenches from sentry posts. I remember an observation post in a tree being deduced from the shadows of two trees on a pond. Dugouts could be detected by the presence of " spoil " in unusual degree, small " nicks " near the entrances, and often by tracks leading overground and had to be distinguished from mine shafts. Battery positions were naturally a subject of lively interest, and it was even possible to distinguish between howitzers and guns by study of the blastmarks on the ground in front; between guns firing under camouflage, batteries in houses, woods, open country, or in cottage ruins, and mere dummy emplacements, or again emplacements for anti-aircraft guns. Photographs taken after a fall of snow were sometimes very tell-tale. During semi-open warfare photos were specially studied for indications of " consolidated " shell-holes, and shell-holes in process of being linked up, tracks leading to woods or battery positions. When one had advanced or retreated out of the area of large-scale maps photographs could be used instead, and I have often found my way across unknown country with their aid, but all officers should know how to use this valuable branch of field-intelligence work—perhaps nowadays they do.

About the month of January it became impossible to replace the casualties in the Brigade at a rate sufficient to maintain the company and Battalion organization and the 110th Brigade, like the rest, had to be reduced to three battalions. Our 9th Battalion was accordingly sacrificed and distributed among the other depleted battalions,—the firstfruit of our activity the previous year in " Killing Germans "— and henceforth we had to base our arrangements on a three-battalion organization, making the relief of the battalions in the trenches much more difficult, as only one battalion could now be out of the line at a time. Thus when the Germans began their last great throw of the dice on March 21st our left flank battalion (the 7th Leicesters) had been on duty in the front line during a period of anxiety and suspense for more than twenty days.

The German Staffs had profited by the experiences of Verdun, the Somme and Ypres, and the preparation of their great offensive in March was both organized and concealed in a masterly manner. As early as January our depleted numbers and totally inadequate reserves, and our knowledge of the masses of enemy reserves released from the Russian front, made the conclusion inevitable that a great attack was in preparation, and when in February I happened to be on leave at a time when Mr. Bonar Law professed to be "very sceptical" that anything would happen and that our line was anyhow safe, I remember being asked my opinion by a pessimistic relation as to whether Paris might be in danger and replying that at least Amiens was. But our foreknowledge was mainly guesswork, confirmed nearer the date by prisoners' statements, and no advertisement was given by the enemy in the form of artillery registration or preliminary bombardment.

Complete concealment was, however, impossible, and danger signals began to appear early in March. From my observation post on the east edge of Epehy village I commanded several long stretches of the great Cambrai–St. Quentin main road behind the enemy lines running between Aubencheul and Bantouzelle, which being several miles behind the line was freely used in day light by their transport, and from about March 10th this traffic, especially of lorries, began to grow prodigiously. Simultaneously new lines of flashing white posts became visible each day, indicating miles of overhead telegraph wires, and I was startled one morning to observe what appeared to be a prisoners of war cage under construction! I made vain efforts to interest the Corps artillery and have the long range 6-inch mark XIX guns turned on my favourite road, especially the vicinity of a house called Rancourt Farm, which from the frequent visits of wagons we surmised to be a dump. Months later a copy of the orders of the German Division—I think the 202nd—which had attacked our Brigade, was taken and found to contain instructions that supplies of ammunition should be drawn from the main divisional dump at Rancourt Farm.

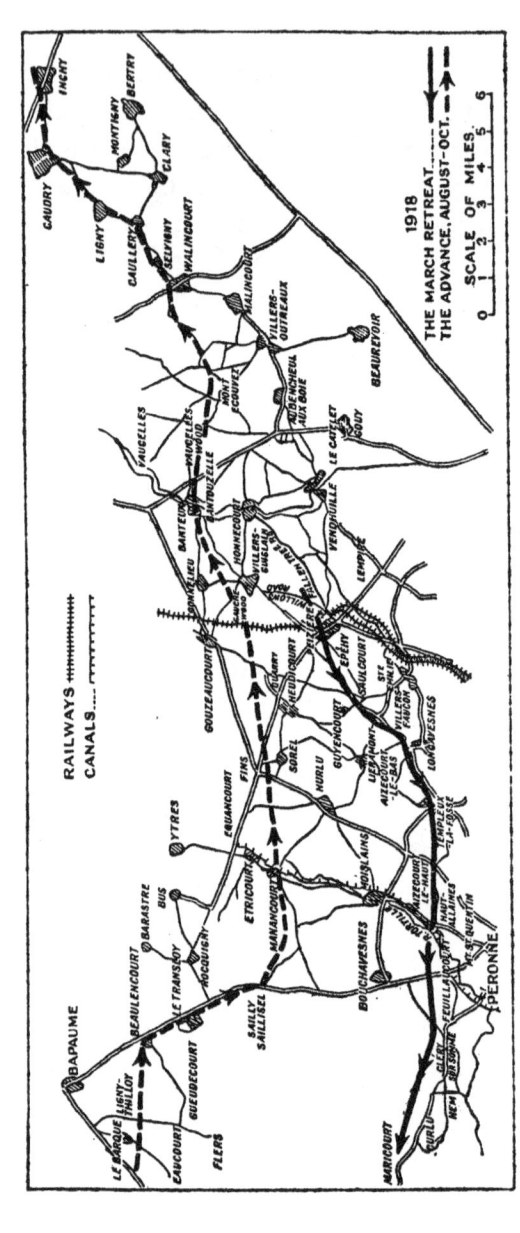

CHAPTER IX

MARCH, 1918

THE last week before March 21st arrived, and the days succeeded each other in ominous calm, but enlivened by a series of clear statements by prisoners which finally crystallized into a definite assurance that the day would be either the 20th or 21st. Brigade headquarters continued to be in cupola shelters in the bank of the mostly sunken road from Saulcourt to Peizières (the name of one end of Epehy), and further down the same road new dugouts were occupied by the headquarters of our left battalion, the 7th, in preparation for the battle.

On the morning of the 20th I escorted as far as these headquarters a young American officer, who had just arrived to be attached for a few days to the Brigade, and entrusted him to the commanding officer. He asked me on the way with an astonished air if it was always so quiet; his question was rudely answered before another night was passed. After the usual chat with whatever officers of the Battalion headquarters were present, I walked on down the road to Peizières, and, entering the village, spent ten minutes with my observers on their platform behind a wall, watching through the telescope the transport on the distant road and the ominous lines of telegraph posts. After visiting the right (8th) Battalion headquarters in a deep dugout in Epehy village (known as " Fishers Keep "), I crossed the great railway cutting on the east side of the village, and made my usual tour of the trenches, talking with sentries, snipers and officers on duty, and here and there visiting Company headquarters in their respective dugouts—my usual morning programme. The air of Sabbath calm was uncanny, and the feeling of spring in the air helped to make the whole situation seem unreal.

General Cayley had left the Brigade the day before, and General Cumming, who had replaced him, had barely time to make the acquaintance of the commanding officers before the storm burst. Everything possible with our limited numbers and too great extent of line had been done to prepare for the shock. Besides the new Battalion headquarters already referred to, a new reserve line of trenches (the " Yellow Line ") had been built west of Epehy-Peizières, and a new dugout made there for the headquarters of the reserve battalion (the 6th) while the telephone cables to the 7th and 8th Battalions had been buried six feet deep, and held good through the first day. That evening I went to sleep for the last time in the little cupola which had been my home for three months, fully dressed and equipped, and at 2.30 a.m. awoke to the sound of an all-pervading pandemonium, which for a few seconds seemed to my half-awake consciousness to be the propellers of a ship. It was the incessant thud of shells on every side. In another second I was in the sunken road outside of my cupola and could have no more doubt that " the day " had come. Our whole area, and all the areas to north and south, were being flooded with high explosive and shrapnel shells, the former falling in serried ranks, with concentrated fire on all roads and trenches in front of us, while an incessant stream of shells whistled over our heads to the transport routes and camps, including the ruined village of Saulcourt behind us.

Soon after dawn detailed news began to arrive from the battalions that masses of enemy infantry were advancing in " snake formation". Our front line was evacuated according to plan, but the first line of resistance (" Fir support ") put up a stout resistance, and was not definitely held by the enemy till the afternoon. At one moment parties of the enemy came through on our left into the village of Peizières itself, but were driven out by the reserve company of the 7th Battalion, aided by two tanks which had lain for a week concealed behind the village on a grassy bank. Our artillery, hopelessly out-numbered and smothered with gas and heavy-calibre shells, stuck to their guns, but the repeated destruction of their telephone lines made it impossible to give them targets or for themselves to observe their own fire. So during the afternoon our infantry had to watch columns of German infantry coming forward in fours, with guns, transport and mounted officers as though on a field day. Fresh attacks were delivered on our main line of resistance (the "Red Line") along the east edge of Epehy village, but were repulsed.

At about 7 p.m. I was asked to visit the three Battalions and collect personal reports on the situation. The whole area had been transformed during the day, the green weedy fields were everywhere torn up with fresh shell-holes, and the air was reeking with gas in many places. As I started out the enemy artillery resumed their fire with fresh vigour to stop possible supplies or reinforcements coming up under cover of darkness, and part of the way down the road to the 7th Battalion I had to run hard. The Battalion headquarters had been shelled out of their new dugout, and were sitting in a slit about a hundred yards away. Having seen the Colonel, I went on into Peizières, visiting our posts on the way, and hugging the walls of the main street which was being swept by occasional bullets, indicating that the enemy were working round our right flank through the 16th Division. Arrived at "Fisher's Keep", the headquarters of the 8th Battalion, I spent half an hour with Colonel Utterson and his Adjutant Spencer-Smith. Soon after I had left, the former was captured and the latter, a cheery "good-mixer", I think from the West Coast of South America, was killed. Tierens, the medical officer of the 6th Battalion came in and told us his aid-post in the south end of the village was in German hands, and that he had been taken prisoner, but released by his captors when they saw his Red Cross armband. About 9.30 p.m. he and I left the 8th Battalion, and started off to look for the 6th (reserve) Battalion in the desolate fields behind Epehy.

It was now pitch-dark, big shells were soughing through the air and crashing down one could not say exactly where. Neither of us was familiar with the ground, and consequently it was not till 11 p.m. that we found the Battalion headquarters. I think the moon had risen. That it should have taken an hour and a half to do what might have been done in a third of the time by daylight illustrates the variety of war. Colonel Stewart's report of the situation was gloomy. The whole of our right flank which had been formed by the 16th Division, appeared to be "in the air", and the great Epehy–St. Emillie road was infested by enemy patrols. The 6th Battalion had too few men to form a defensive flank, for they had lost heavily from shell-fire and the process was still going on. The dugout was full of wounded, some terribly mutilated. About midnight I took my leave of Colonel Stewart, who had always been a very good friend, for the last time. He was shot down by a sniper in front of his headquarters a few hours later.

About 7 a.m. I was ordered to proceed as liaison officer to the troops of the reserve Division (I think the 39th) who had been thrown into battle on our right flank to reinforce the 16th Division. As there was no telephone communication on this flank I took two orderlies and made my way along the "Brown Line" (a reserve trench running past our Brigade headquarters and already garrisoned by a miscellaneous array of our Brigade headquarter personnel, a company of R.E.'s, and our trench-mortar men), to a quarry on the Epehy-St. Emillie road, where I found a battalion of the Hertfordshire Regiment. The banks of the half-surrounded quarry were lined with a miscellaneous group mostly Battalion headquarter personnel, who kept the enemy at bay and drove off several half-hearted attacks. Unfortunately, one of our own batteries was shooting into our midst; there were about fifty casualties, many due to this. I sent off first one and then the other orderly with reports, and stayed with the Hertfords for the return of one of my orderlies with instructions, but in the meantime events were moving fast, unknown to me, in our Brigade area. For my own Brigade, acting on orders from the Division, had successively evacuated the Red Line, Epehy village, the Yellow Line and finally the Brown Line and the Brigade headquarter shelters, the mass of the troops finally retiring through Saulcourt back to Longavesnes with the Brigade headquarters staff. Neither of my orderlies reached the headquarters, and what happened to them I never knew. Rearguards fought obstinately in Epehy to cover the retreat; Captain Maclay of the 6th Battalion, one of our best Company commanders, was killed there, and I heard that the streets were full of German dead. In the Brown Line, by which I had come to the Quarry, the miscellaneous garrison were mostly cut off through ignorance of the general retirement, and our Brigade headquarter cook and mess-waiter were taken prisoners while Captain Lawson who commanded our light trench-mortar battery was killed.

All this, however, was unknown to me at the time, and I remained with the Hertfords awaiting the return of an orderly. At 1 p.m. the Hertfords finding themselves nearly encircled, and without instructions, decided to retire through Villers-Faucon, so I left them and set out to regain my Brigade headquarters, which I still believed to be where I had left it. I was soon undeceived. As I approached our old Brown Line I was greeted by direct fire with rifles and machine-guns from groups of Germans in the trench. Had they not fired, I suppose nothing could have saved me from being shot or taken, as had doubtless been the fate of my messengers. Plunging into a shallow unfinished trench which ran towards Saulcourt, I crawled along it, each time I showed myself drawing a burst of machine-gun fire. After about two hundred yards of this I grew desperate, and resolved to make a dash for the Villers-Faucon-Saulcourt road. Jumping out I ran across the open for three or four hundred yards under the direct and concentrated fire of several machine-guns till I reached dead ground close to Villers-Faucon, and sat gasping for breath for about four minutes. It had been a near thing and a most unpleasant sensation. Walking on to Saulcourt village I gradually realized the full gravity of the situation and by a fortunate inspiration turned towards Longavesnes, hitherto our Divisional headquarters. I arrived there some time before 3 p.m., and was delighted to find the Battalions and Brigade staff, who professed to have given me up.

Within about half an hour we were on the move again, withdrawing through Templeux-la-Fosse (hitherto the headquarters of the VIIth Corps) to Aizecourt-le-Haut, where the Brigade occupied a line of wide unfinished trenches. Headquarters spent the night in a hut. At about 4 a.m. next morning (the 23rd), having had a meal—the last one I was to get till 11 p.m.—I set off with Captain Leake, the Brigade bombing officer, to visit the troops whose trenches were about a mile and a quarter distant. In places the wide shallow trenches were hardly more than a trace, and we found nearly everyone asleep, as was hardly surprising. As we were returning a German barrage began to come down, and as the attack developed our troops withdrew without waiting for it to a new line running east and north-east of Aizecourt. About 10 a.m. I went to Haut-Allaines camp, and returned to the line by Aizecourt with a limber containing smallarms ammunition. While the wagon was being unloaded we saw a wave of Germans walking across a field on our flank : the unloading party lined a ditch and opened fire. What struck me was that no one took this obvious action till an order had been given, a curious illustration of the cramping effect of prolonged trench-warfare.

By 11 a.m. the troops were evacuating Aizecourt and streaming back by Haut-Allaines and Aizecourt-le-bas to the Peronne canal. I joined a mixed column containing elements of all our three Brigades, and commanded by General Gator of the 62nd Brigade, as the senior officer present. We crossed the canal by a bridge in a village, then re-forming moved up on to a ridge dominating the canal-crossing, and occupied an ancient trench. Another column, mostly composed of my own Brigade crossed further north under Colonel Sawyer of the 7th Leicesters, while the remainder of the Division retired further south, I think by way of Feuillaucourt. We were now back on the edge of the old Somme battlefield, utterly deserted since April, 1917. All around stretched the old wilderness of shell-holes, mostly overgrown with grass. At our feet lay the canal, on the further side of which the German vanguards were already in view, but halted on coming under direct fire from two solitary field guns. South of us we could see the towering hill of Mount St. Quentin, the ownership of which was a matter of speculation. Neither to right nor to left of us were any British troops to be seen. Presently my own Brigadier arrived on foot: he had visited the 64th Brigade staff at Feuillaucourt, and returning through the village, by which we had just crossed the canal, found German patrols in it and galloped for his life. His horse carried him out of range and then dropped dead.

Having decided certain questions of policy he instructed me to go to Feuillaucourt where he had left our Staff captain with the 64th Brigade staff, to inform him where we were, what we proposed to do, and to arrange about the rations. I accordingly set out with Captain Leake—it was now about 12.30 p.m.—and striking the old Mount St. Quentin-Bouchavesnes high road—a typical Somme road with its stunted dead poplars and endless vision of shell-holes to right and left—turned down towards Feuillaucourt on the canal. Taught by experience we approached warily, and when within a few hundred yards of the village, where our Staff captain was supposed to be, saw the now familiar field grey uniforms moving about freely in it. There was not an English soldier to be seen in any direction, and the miserable landscape offered little encouragement. However, we knew our Divisional headquarters had been intended to be at the village of Clery, further south, so after some anxious map-reading—for a miscalculation might lead us among the enemy at any minute—we started to move south again. We went another mile before encountering any English troops, and formed the impression that at that moment there was a clear gap in the line of about three miles. Happily the enemy took no advantage of this situation. I have often wondered whether the well-stocked canteens we had abandoned had anything to do with this. They must have been a sore temptation. The first friends we found were some of the 64th Brigade with Colonel McCulloch of the K.O.Y.L.I. At about 4 p.m., as we were approaching the village of Clery, lying along a deep sunken main road, a flight of enemy aeroplanes came overhead, and seeing a tank and some wagons close to us, swooped down to within two hundred feet of us and opened machine-gun fire. For several anxious minutes we lay in shell-holes, while bullets hit the ground all round us, and I had a vivid impression of a round-faced aviator with a dark moustache leaning over the side and apparently taking aim at me. It was one of the few occasions when I felt a severe hatred of an individual member of the enemy army, but one has a peculiar sense of impotence when attacked by an aeroplane. As had happened the day before, I grew impatient, and made a dash for the road, sliding down the bank and jumping into an open cellar among the ruins of the village. Strange to say, only a couple of horses were killed.

In a sunken road off the main street I found—after the aeroplanes had gone—the 64th Brigade staff. They told me the Divisional staff had gone, but had left a telephonist. Arrived at the abandoned Divisional headquarters we found that the telephonist had also disappeared, but were consoled by finding on the floor a half-empty tin of apricot jam, which we speedily finished with our fingers, having had a strenuous morning's exercise since our meal at 3.30

a.m., and as I had lost my water-bottle overnight. Though the conception of the " Chocolate Soldier " was a little exaggerated, I think that at any rate for a staff officer a water-bottle is as important as a revolver. At this moment we were overjoyed to encounter our motor-cycle dispatch-rider, one of those remarkable men who seem always to turn up at the right place. He gave us an inestimable drink from his water-bottle, and told us where to find our Staff captain and what remained of our Brigade transport—part of which, including our headquarters mess-cart, with all our stores, had been cut off by the Germans at Peronne that morning. It seemed an artistic finish to the capture of our cook and waiter the day before. At about 7 p.m. we set off to find the location he had given us, and after an hour and a half's steady walking came upon our horse lines and the Staff captain. The latter on receiving our information set off at once with the rations, and though the troops had in fact " side-slipped " several miles from where we had left them and were by that time somewhere near Clery, he succeeded in finding them.

At about 3.30 a.m. Leake and I, having learned approximately the new position of the troops set out to rejoin them. From 4 to 5 we wandered amid the trackless wilderness of shell-holes, finding only isolated groups of other units, until following a clue given by one of these we went down into Clery, and found the 64th Brigade staff again: this time in the western end of the village. Helped by a dense fog the Germans began to attack, and as they entered the east end of the village, we walked away from the other end. The next village going west along the road was Hem, and here in some huts close to Clery-Maricourt main road we found all three Brigadiers assembled, and learned that our infantry were holding some old trenches on a ridge some eighteen hundred yards to the north. One of the huts was a derelict Y.M.C.A. canteen, where the 64th Brigade Mess corporal found an abundant supply of tinned milk and fruit, to my great gratification, as I had had nothing since the night before. Speaking again of the comparative values of water-bottles and revolvers, I should mention that all ranks were supposed to carry an emergency ration, but I always dispensed with this, and any other equipment not absolutely necessary, in order to be able to travel light and therefore faster, my duties being of a different order to those of the regimental officer.

Early in the afternoon I was sent to order our troops to evacuate their positions on the ridge and retire in a westerly direction. The sporting Leake again voluntarily accompanied me, and together we wandered over the crest, frequently obliged to crawl or run as snipers or machine-gunners opened fire on us from unexpected directions. Eventually we realized that we were absolutely alone, except for a solitary tank which was working up over the crest and disappeared into Nomansland—I suppose its commander had also received out-of-date instructions, and we never saw what became of him or his tank. For in fact Colonel Sawyer, with whom was the Brigade Major, had found his left flank was entirely in the air and anticipating the orders I was to convey had evacuated the area an hour earlier. Had the Germans been advancing in a less leisurely manner my companion and I would certainly have had a bad quarter of an hour.

Eventually our Division was relieved by the 35th Division, of which one Brigade had already come up to reinforce our right flank, and we fell back via Maricourt to Bray. The Brigade staff took charge of a composite force made up of Labour corps, men from leave collected at the base, and stragglers from a very reduced Scottish Division. This variegated team dug in hastily between Ribemont and Sailly-le-Sec, but the German advance had been definitely checked, and by the end of March the staff had rejoined the Brigade, now re-formed and rested, at Allonville. We immediately entrained by night from Amiens *en route* for Flanders once more. At this time the enemy aircraft were visiting Amiens almost every night, and especially bombed St. Roch station, but we were fortunate in escaping their attentions when we entrained there on the night of April 1st–2nd. Our casualties as a Brigade in the battle had been thirty-one officers and about twelve hundred men out of a very much weaker Brigade than that which had fought on the Somme. We had it will be remembered, already lost one battalion, and the three that were left were below strength, so we must have lost about half our effectives. On the other hand, we had undoubtedly taken a heavy toll of the enemy, as the prolonged check of the advance in front of Epehy (specially referred to in a German communiqué) would alone be sufficient to indicate.

CHAPTER X

APRIL, 1918
(SEE MAP FACING PAGE 75)

WE detrained at a military railway-station in Flanders known as " Hop out R.E." (which I at first took for a genuine Flemish name and pronounced " Hopootre "), and for several days engaged in one of those *chassé-croisé* exercises so familiar in the War, our Brigade group with all its transport touring round a small area like a circus. We spent a night in the village of Locre which we had last seen in July, 1915, when we first came to France, and another in a camp of huts near by known as " Faery House ". All this Flemish back area, which had remained intact throughout the War, was destined to be laid waste within a week or two. There was an idea that we should take over the Messines–Wytschaet ridge, and I visited that area, but the project was abandoned. The Second Army Commander, General Plumer, came to visit us and delivered a short address to the officers. The chief points of the address were that there was no prospect of a German offensive in these parts, and that we must seize the opportunity of being in a quiet sector to recuperate and get fit again.

The advice sounded strange a few days later when the German offensive in Flanders was in full swing, but the Army Commander may have been right on strategic principles.

On the 9–10th April our Brigade relieved the 148th Brigade of the 49th Division in the trenches south of the Menin road, which included the ridge called Tower Hamlets, and were approached through the miserable swamp called Dumbarton Wood. The area included also on the right the blasted wood called Shrewsbury Forest; on our immediate left lay the battlefield we had held in October.

Though complete calm reigned at the moment, it was a difficult area to get about in : even in good weather one could hardly move off the wooden tracks, so sodden and spongy were the edges of the ubiquitous shell-holes. Dumbarton Wood, where every tree had had a direct hit by a shell, was a particularly eerie sight, and the whole landscape presented a dreary and indeed disgusting spectacle. Our left front battalion had a curious position out in front of the Bassevillebeck, once a brook but now a swamp, passable only in Indian file by a single track. The only attractive feature was the existence of some large mined dugouts, particularly one called Torr Top, about two thousand yards behind the front line, which played an important part in the subsequent operations. The sector had become so quiet that the Brigade headquarters were in totally unprotected huts in the open alongside the wooden " Warrington

Road" which ran past Zillebeke Lake, a favourite location for our batteries.

On the very morning of the 9th we had listened for many hours to a terrific artillery concentration on our right, indicating the German attack on La Bassée, which soon threatened to eclipse their successes on 21st March. As the offensive developed on the Lys, our batteries round Zillebeke Lake began to shoot at the flank of the advancing enemy, who began to give us some of his attention in consequence and on the morning of the 10th the area between our Brigade headquarters and our most advanced field batteries began to be shelled. At one time an attack on our trenches was anticipated and I went to Torr Top, with the idea of establishing a forward headquarters, but it proved unnecessary.

As the enemy attack to the south developed, threatening eventually to encircle us and take the whole Ypres salient in the rear, it was decided to withdraw secretly the main body of the British troops in the salient, while maintaining an outpost line to delay the enemy. In accordance with this scheme our Brigade on the 15th fell back to new positions along the Ypres–St. Eloi road, between the Lille gate of Ypres and the village of Voormezeele, but leaving one isolated battalion in trenches east of Torr Top, and nearly three kilometres east of Zillebeke Lake. Thus these rearguard troops had no one behind them till one came to the new front line about three miles back, and the new Brigade headquarters

APRIL, 1918

were six miles behind them. The staff were glad to see the last of the huts on Warrington Road, where for several days and nights we had worked, eaten and slept with high velocity shells intermittently screaming overhead, and frequently plunging down a hundred yards in front, between us and Zillebeke Lake. It was unpleasant to reflect that the slightest shortening of the range would cause our huts to disappear.

Our new headquarters were in huts under the lee of a solitary farmhouse north-west of Dickebusch, known as Walker Camp. Hitherto a back area to the Ypres salient, this country was full of light railways built in 1917, and as the roads were now frequently under fire from long-range guns I found the railway lines useful to walk on in my visits to the new defence line which we were feverishly constructing. The difficulties began when it came to walking on through the area we had just evacuated to visit the rearguard outpost line which we maintained right up to the night of the 26–27th. Through this deserted terrain one walked for nearly half an hour without meeting a single human being, and in the evening the Very lights seemed to be flaring in a circle all round. The Battalion headquarters and most of the officers were in Torr Top dugout, and as the entrances to it were under enemy observation and accurately shelled, the approach was a tricky business. On one occasion I ran the last twenty yards in what must have been an athletic record to get in between two of a succession of light shells which were falling right on the only possible track. At any moment the enemy might have broken through with comparative ease, and hardly anyone of this unsupported rearguard could have escaped, so their nervous tension can be imagined.

On the 25th a fresh German attack developed south of us and swept over the dominating height of Mount Kemmel itself, and on to within a mile of the Dickebusch–La Clytte road, resulting in the extraordinary situation that our Brigade headquarters was within two miles of the advancing enemy on our flank while remaining nearly six miles behind our forward battalion on what was still our front. We were once more living among the batteries firing in enfilade on to the battle front, and became in consequence exposed to heavy counter-battery fire. We abandoned our huts—several of which were blown to bits immediately after—and took refuge under the brick walls of the farmhouse, hastily strengthened by sand-bags. The cook-house, in a lean-to against the farmhouse wall, received a direct hit from a gas-shell and one shell came through the roof of our own farmhouse, which otherwise remained almost miraculously intact for, owing to the strange geographical situation, we had shells coming overhead from almost all directions. Dickebusch had till recently been so far behind the line that there was still an elderly Y.M.C.A. official there who gallantly refused to quit and on the 24th had gone with our mess-cart to Poperinghe and bought stores for us and presumably for other units. On the next day Dickebusch was an inferno of heavy shells, and I wondered what had become of him, but never saw him again.

The situation on our right that morning (the 25th) being obscure I set out towards La Clytte and Kemmel to gather information. The road from Ouderdom to Groote-Vierstraat, especially the crossroads called Hallebast Corner, and indeed all the roads and tracks, were being very heavily shelled, black spouts of earth seeming to spring up continuously in every direction, though in a sufficiently regular manner to enable an experienced traveller to dodge through. I had conversation with the staff of another Brigade, with some officers of a French battalion, and an observer from the 64th Brigade who was looking for his own headquarters, and managed to fit the different accounts together. My report conflicted with that of another unit, but was confirmed in due course.

That evening the enemy began to feel his way along the banks of the Ypres–Commines canal, which our new front line bestrode where two bridges crossed it just north of Voormezeele, and it became evident that our exposed rearguard line out in the old salient must be immediately brought back. On the afternoon of the 26th, therefore, I started off with orders for their retirement. As I trudged the last kilometre or more along the track to Torr Top I had a creepy feeling from the knowledge that on my right there was presumably no one between myself and the

Germans, but it was a consolation to witness the relief of the marooned garrison of Torr Top on whom the strain of their unprecedented position was beginning to tell. That night the Battalion got back safely to the main body, and the Germans came through next morning.

Our newly-prepared front line, especially round the Ypres–Commines canal, now became very disagreeable. It comprised a trench system and a number of strong-points round ruined buildings such as those known to us as " Bedford House " and " Lankhof Farm," and both trenches and strong-points were now constantly shelled, both with heavy shells and murderous concentrations of gas; sometimes it was necessary to wear gas masks for four or five hours continuously. The chief Battalion headquarters was in dugouts under a tall, gaunt ruin south of Ypres, called Swan Château. It was constantly shelled, and a direct hit from a really heavy shell would probably have buried all the inmates, but in that region dugouts of any sort were rare, and priceless, as some sleep was possible for those inside. It is a curious fact that those with roving commissions like myself developed from constant practice a sort of instinct as to how to approach such places; many times I have had the feeling that out of two alternative tracks one in particular was about to be shelled, or that a particular hour would be quiet or dangerous for the pedestrian, and these inspirations were frequently justified. Usually the most unpleasant experiences occurred when circumstances prevented one from choosing his own time and route of approach. Partly this may have been some revival of natural instinct; war brings one very close to earth.

On the night of the 27–28th one whole company posted near the canal at " Lankhof Farm " disappeared during a German raid. It was the twentieth day of this interminable battle, of which the chief characteristic was the lack of shelter which made sleep difficult, and it was assumed that this unfortunate company had been too exhausted to keep awake. Next day our neighbours on our immediate right were attacked and lost Woormezeele, which left our right flank in greater danger than ever, while at the same time the shell-fire grew still heavier all over our area. On the 29th our posts on the canal by the " Iron Bridge ", were attacked during the afternoon but held firm, and as our artillery was now again holding its own, and the enemy were as badly off for shelter as ourselves, their casualties were presumably growing out of proportion to their gains. On some occasion during this period I visited neighbouring units in dugouts under, or close to, the famous " Hill 60 " which is still preserved as a specimen of what the whole of that countryside looked like in 1918. This period marked the definite arrival of an intensified phase of the War. In 1915, and till much later in " normal " sectors, the relatively safe back area was supposed to extend to within two or three thousand yards of the front line, but now one only began to feel safe at five thousand yards and continued for double that distance to be within range of numerous long-range guns. Now also enfilade fire, which has a most disturbing moral effect, became a regular practice of the Germans, who adopted the tactical maxim that guns were best employed when firing to a flank rather than to their front. In April, owing to our being at the apex of a lengthening salient, our transport lines, though several hours' journey from our own Brigade front, were much nearer other portions of the British front, and had to be constantly shifted to avoid shell-fire. In fact for all practical purposes we had no " back area " at all during this month. My own walks became rather an obsession, as I never knew when I should not have to start off by day or night at a minute's notice to " go up the line ", though indeed our farmhouse was not itself a haven of rest. The corner of it in which we lived—for it was a mere cottage and such as it was had to be shared with our numerous personnel of signallers, and runners—was incessantly crowded with visitors seeking information, artillery liaison officers, and temporarily attached signal officers, and while the Brigade Major was incessantly telephoning or writing orders, I was kept busy with maps, reports and all sorts of details. One lived in a crowd, which is always detestable and would have welcomed any opportunity to get away for a few hours if prolonged walking in that area had not been so excessively dangerous. Consequently it was with a special sense of pleasure that I welcomed our relief by the 58th Brigade of the 19th Division on the night of April 30th to May 1st, and I have seldom left any place with less regret than that wretched farmhouse at Walker Camp. Civil life affords no thrill comparable to the primitive satisfaction one felt on such occasions on returning to relatively decent quarters and the prospect of a bath and a few days' rest, and I think that this particular thrill from the mere sense of relative peace and quiet is one of the things which if only for its psychological interest one should not be so apt to forget. All one's senses were as if heightened and rendered more acute, and I am quite certain that civilized life has no pleasures akin to these elemental sensations.

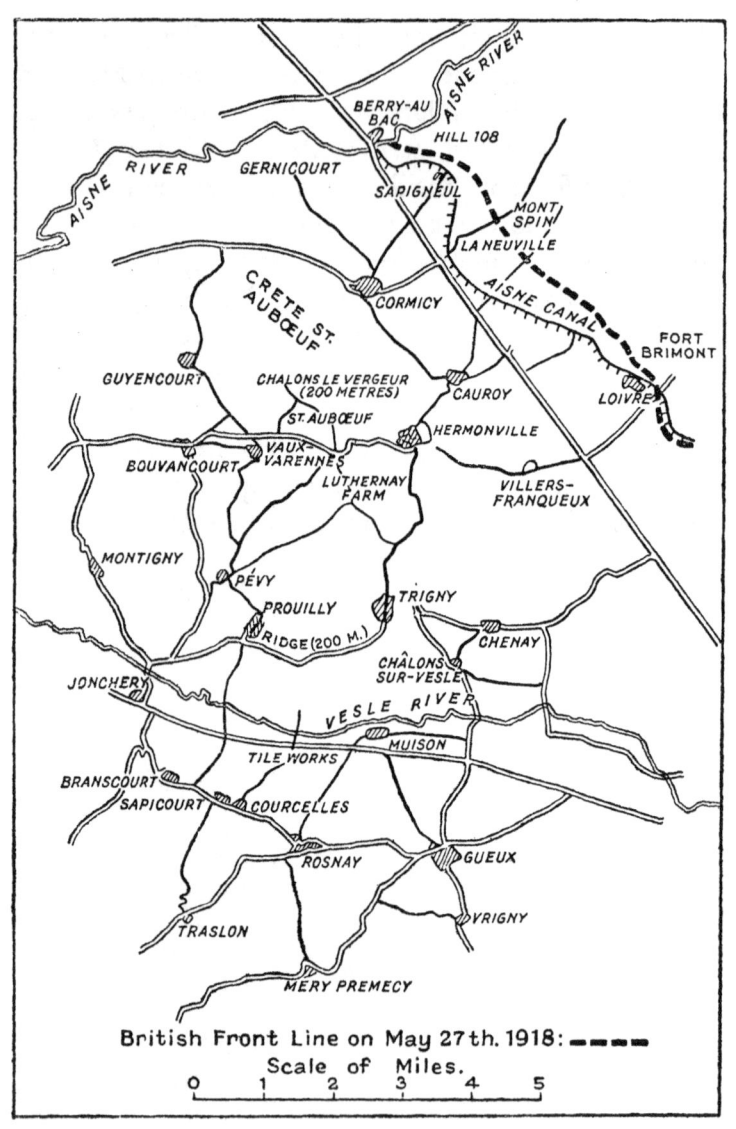

CHAPTER XI

MAY, 1918

THE Brigade marched away by way of Cassel, passing masses of French infantry and guns on their way into the battle, with trains of queer, high-piled carts of all descriptions drawn by long-maned horses always trotting when not in column. Half the staffs of the Second Army seemed to be lunching in the Sauvage Inn on the summit of Cassel, with its views of the sea and Mount Kemmel. We entrained from Wizernes and on May 6th arrived in the area of the 6th French Army, which had undertaken to provide a rest-cure for four battered British Divisions composing the IX Corps. We spent a few days in the village of Lagery, where, thanks to the presence of an energetic French Town Major, every man had a mattress. From here we passed through Pevy to the 38th French Corps, and our Division relieved the 74th French Division in the angle made by the Aisne River with the Aisne canal. Our own Brigade relieved, on the 14–15th May, the 230 French Regiment (Chasseurs Alpins) in the " Chalons-le-Vergeur " sector.

The forward area of this sector was a chalk plain intersected by the Aisne canal; our front line, unfortunately as it proved, ran east of the canal, at one point as much as fifteen hundred metres beyond it. This forward area lay at the foot of a magnificent densely-wooded ridge, the Crete St. Aubœuf, on which, completely concealed by the wood, lay the Regimental headquarters. These consisted of chambers cut into a bank, with pleasant rustic terraces and gardens laid out by the servants. One path led to a charming little timber chapel made with rustic elegance for the French regimental chaplain. Before the relief I visited the regiment with the Brigadier, and we were regaled with a sumptuous lunch, with much popping of champagne corks and drinking of healths. As we were studying the maps before lunch the mess waiter had announced solemnly "*Madame est servie*", and on being asked by the old Colonel "*qu'est ce qu'tu nous fous com'ratatouille aujourd'hui*", declaimed the menu in a sort of ecclesiastical chant. Conversation was most animated and amusing, ranging on all sorts of general topics, and the youngest present did not seem to be in the least awed by the old Colonel and the other seniors; all of which would have thrown some of our senior officers into a fit.

The sector seemed indeed to promise a rest-cure, and my "opposite number", the French regimental Intelligence Officer, Lieutenant Westphal, explained to me that the established custom was to fire two shots if the enemy fired one, but otherwise to let sleeping dogs lie, and one of the first things I noticed was

MAY, 1918

that the telephone wires were merely carried along the trenches, instead of being buried as was our usual practice. Apart from the intense heat, the conditions seemed delightful, but there were tactical features which caused us disquiet. The canal with its deep two hundred metres marsh would have made an excellent front line, but as it ran close to the front line of our neighbours on the flank it would, so long as we remained out in front of it, enable the enemy to walk along it and so surround our front line troops, which in fact was what happened. Moreover the whole area was under view from the enemy heights, Hill 108, Mont Spin and the Great Fort Brimont. To remedy this the French had screened all roads and tracks with high nets for many miles, an organization I had never seen before. On our left lay the Chemin des Dames.

On the 22nd I went on leave to Paris for two days, having had a slight attack of " flu ", and returning to P.C. Savoie, on the night of the 25th, was jocularly informed by the Brigade Major that my observers had been " putting the wind up the Corps " by reporting that they had seen long strings of horses, apparently gun-teams, returning at dawn from the enemy forward areas. Next day I spent a long time at my observation post, and watched the disturbing spectacle of enemy linesmen laying out new telephone wires. I was therefore not surprised to learn on returning to Brigade headquarters that a telegram had just come stating that deserters taken by the

French XIth Corps had predicted a general attack on our front at one a.m. of the following morning (the 27th).

At a minute to one next morning our signal officer called up all our Battalions in order to test the lines. At one o'clock precisely a terrific drum-fire with a large proportion of gas-shells crashed like an avalanche all over our area, and when a minute later the signal officer tested the lines again there was no reply—every cable had already been cut by direct hits into the trenches. As the shelling went on steadily hour after hour communication could never be restored, and all information had to be by messenger. I spent several hours at an artillery observation post, but could see nothing as there was a fog till about 8 a.m., and merely swallowed a quantity of gas. The enemy attack probably developed between 3 and 4 a.m., but as our isolated companies east of the treacherous canal were annihilated we never knew exactly. Throughout the morning our battalions fought hard in the area between the Cauroy–Cormicy road and the canal; the area east of the canal, and the near bank of the canal itself, were certainly lost by 7 a.m. One strong point, the " Tenaille de Guise ", held out till 3 p.m. My observers, whose post was near the headquarters of the right battalion, got away as usual just in time, having lost nothing but a pair of my field-glasses which had been buried by a direct hit from a shell. I have the greatest admiration for the conscientious and intelligent manner in which my observers always carried out their lonely and often responsible duties, and have been glad to have the opportunity in the course of this narrative to record some indisputable cases of the value of their work.

When the fog lifted we could see from the top of St. Aubœuf ridge what was going on, and later could observe a stream of enemy reinforcements coming up to a wood, the " Bois Allongé ", close to my observation post, and emerging from thence in small parties to renew their attacks. Meanwhile the enemy had been making startling progress away on our left, on the Chemin des Dames, and we received verbal orders for a complete withdrawal after nightfall to a new line continuing the St. Aubœuf ridge in a south-westerly direction and running east of the Hermonville–Bouvancourt road, in all about fourteen hundred yards being assigned to the Brigade. I went over with the Staff captain to mark out our line, and finding some already prepared trenches, we sat down to await the battalions and guide them to their respective sections.

According to the theory on which the orders were based, this portion was to be part of a new line, to be continued by the 8th Division on our left past Bouvancourt, on our right by a French battalion and the 25th Division. Brigade headquarters were to be at Vaux-Varennes, seemingly a suitable position behind the centre of the line. Our surprise can be imagined when just as the battalions were arriving at about midnight and taking up their posts two Germans walked straight into a group consisting of myself and several other officers, and informed us that their fellows were in Bouvancourt, and that they had seen nothing whatever of the 8th British Division which we imagined to be covering our left flank and holding Bouvancourt. I walked to Vaux-Varennes, intended to be our Brigade headquarters, and there found that news had just arrived that German patrols were actually behind that village, and barring our line of communication and retreat through Pevy, indicated in our orders as the Divisional headquarters. It was therefore obvious that our new Brigade line was completely " in the air " with Germans in unknown numbers miles in the rear of it.

There remained only one possible (though far from certain) way of escape, namely by a circuitous cross-country track south-west of Hermonville to Pevy, and the Brigadier decided to withdraw along this route and hope for the best. At 3.30 a.m. accordingly the Brigade, formed into one battalion, began its march, in complete silence. As day dawned we halted at Luthernay Farm, where a low-flying enemy aeroplane dropped some bombs; luckily it was solitary. At this time—about 6.30 a.m. I fancy—we received orders from the Division to proceed to Pevy as reserve Brigade, while the 64th and 62nd Brigades were to take up a line south-west of Hermonville. Now, as I have already described, German patrols had been on the road from Vaux-Varennes to

Pevy as early as 1 a.m.; and as it turned out, they must have been actually entering Pevy or on the point of doing so, when we received these orders. It was one more illustration of the difficulty of keeping orders in touch with realities in a war of movement, and of the extent to which officers must rely on their own judgment and initiative in such circumstances. However, we were unaware of the situation at Pevy, and on receiving these orders set off again towards it, with the exception of the 6th Battalion which remained with the 64th Brigade owing to the dispatch-rider, who was taking them their orders for withdrawal, being wounded on the way.

We had arrived—towards 8 a.m.—within perhaps five hundred yards of Pevy when from the heights just above that village, and very close to us, a heavy machine-gun and rifle fire was directed at us. Plainly the village before us was in enemy hands: from the high ground on our right we were being actively shot at: on our left, where the great Prouilly-Trigny ridge offered a way of escape, lay a belt of swamp separating us from the ridge. For the moment it seemed as if our mixed body (for we had large elements of the 62nd Brigade with us) had walked into a trap. There was only one possible hope of safety, and breaking up into a number of columns in single file we plunged into the swamp and headed for the Prouilly ridge, which I remember comparing with Box Hill in Surrey. Wading laboriously through that swamp (where Colonel Sawyer of the 7th Battalion plunged up to his neck) we offered a splendid target to our enemies a few hundred yards away, but owing perhaps to some miscalculation due to the deceptive terrain, most of their bullets went over our heads. The two German prisoners who had given us such valuable, if disconcerting, information a few hours before had been loaded by our Brigade headquarters orderlies with " dixies " and rations, and as they staggered through the water were cursing their late comrades, some of whose bullets were splashing round them. Presently we reached firm ground and began the painful ascent of Prouilly ridge, the summit of which meant temporary security. Our mess waiter, a diminutive youth of nineteen, was carrying an enormous sack of crockery and stores which he had dragged with him through the night, then across the swamp under fire, and finally right up the hillside. It was a remarkable instance of devotion to an unromantic duty, as nobody would have been surprised if he had lost it on the way.

As we were toiling up there appeared over the skyline a wave of French infantry, belonging to a Colonial, but white, regiment. Arrived on the summit we formed up and lined the cliff-tops, forming with the French a complete cordon facing in all directions : where we stayed till 3.30 p.m. It was a glorious morning, the view of the lovely Champagne country —hitherto practically untouched by the War—was superb, the German artillery had not yet come into action, and we spent the morning basking in the sun and enjoying the view. Unfortunately as the day wore on it became evident that our flanks were once more in the air, and we could see German patrols working forward on three sides of us by midday. The German artillery also began to make their presence felt once more—presumably they had had difficulties in getting over the canal and our trenches. A fresh retirement therefore took place, and by nightfall we had crossed the River Vesle several miles further back and had taken up a new position at the tile-works west of Muizon.

Brigade headquarters spent that night (the 28-29th) in a pleasant little village called Rosnay, about forty minutes' walk further back. The main danger continued to threaten from the left flank, where the enemy was still profiting by his tremendous drive North of the Aisne, and early in the morning of the 29th it became evident that instead of attacking us frontally over the river Vesle, he would continue his enveloping tactics, pressing in a south-easterly direction from Jonchery. A detachment under Colonel Chance, strengthened later by troops withdrawn from the tile-works, was therefore sent up to the high ground west of Rosnay, called Hill 202. I accompanied Colonel Chance as a guide to this point, and from there cut across to Sapicourt, where the French filled an important gap, and in the village street found a French company commander with his men behind

I

a barricade. He explained to me that the Germans were attacking him from Branscourt, but that apart from heavy casualties from shell-fire, he was not in serious difficulties.

Just after I returned to Rosnay, that village was suddenly subjected to a crash of German shells, one of which burst in the yard of our house and killed the Staff captain of another Brigade which he said had been practically annihilated. As the house had no cellar, we hastily withdrew to a hill just south of the village. I felt rather hurt when a French officer, to whom I explained, in answer to a question about the village, that we had been shelled out of it, asked how could we expect to check the enemy if we retired every time we were shelled? I could very easily have set his mind at rest by explaining the situation, but as we were conversing from a distance felt too annoyed to do so. It illustrates the danger of judging others too quickly.

That evening Brigade headquarters withdrew to the large village of Mery-Premecy, where we received telephone orders in the estaminet we occupied to the effect that the 45th French Division having come through our line, we could withdraw our men as soon as the Brigadiers were satisfied that the French had taken over. This was at 9 p.m., and our transport being with us I started off on horseback, accompanied at first by representatives of the 64th and 62nd Brigades, on the same mission, to convey this message to Battalion commanders. Riding towards Hill 202

I found that the force holding it had been driven off on to the lower ground and that Colonel Chance himself had been killed by a shell. His adjutant, Captain Tooth, had taken command and I found him sitting in a cellar with a vivacious French major. I then went on through Rosnay, already sadly knocked about by shell-fire, and found Colonel Sawyer, who had been forced back from the Tile Works to within a thousand yards of Rosnay. Sapicourt, where I had found the French company behind their barricade, had also, I found, fallen. Walking back through the deserted village of Rosnay, where there were a number of badly wounded men whom I could do nothing to help, I got back to Mery-Premecy between 1 and 2 a.m., and we started off to Pourcy, where the Brigade halted for three hours. Thence—it being now the 30th—we marched to a clearing in the forest of Epernay, where we bivouacked for the night, and finally on the 31st marched to Etrechy and billeted there.

On the way we passed a pathetic procession of refugees abandoning, with what belongings they could carry, homes where they had dwelt in imagined security since the battles of 1914. I remember in particular a girl pushing a cart loaded with mattresses on the top of which sat perched an aged lady. Our Brigade casualties had been fifty-two officers and thirteen hundred and seventy-eight other ranks, of whom no less than thirty-three officers and eleven hundred and sixty-eight men were missing. We were not yet wholly " out of the wood ", as a composite Brigade, to which each of our three Brigades contributed a mixed battalion, was formed to work with French units on the Marne, but I remember only that the staff of another Brigade was in charge, and there was no further fighting.

CHAPTER XII

THE LAST INTERVAL
(SEE MAP FACING PAGE 27)

ABOUT the middle of June the Division moved to the north coast, and enjoyed several weeks' rest—the first since September, 1917. When one reflects that the intervening period had included the Ypres offensive, the hard winter at Epehy, the March retreat, the three weeks' battle in April, and the May retreat just ended, one has some idea of what was expected of our regiments. During this period of rest our 8th Battalion went the way of the 9th, being reduced to " cadre " and sent home. Now only two Leicestershire battalions remained, but we were joined by the 1st Battalion Wiltshire Regiment. The rest area was pleasant, somewhere in the neighbourhood of Dieppe, and we had our headquarters in the thirteenth-century château of the Marquis de Rambure, whose town house in Abbeville was the well-known officers' club.

The Château of Rambure was the most interesting billet we had during the war. Dating from the thirteenth century, since when it had, I was informed, always been in the same family, it contained a collection of family portraits going back to Renaissance times, and a tapestry which had disappeared at the Revolution, and been recently bought back at a sale in Paris by our host, whose wife told me the companion to it had also been in the market but had been beyond their means. There was a chapel built inside the thickness of one of the walls.

About the middle of July, as the turning point of the War was drawing near, we came down to the Raincheval area and towards the end of the month took over trenches running along the river Ancre, facing the battle-scarred hill of Thiepval. Here, exactly two years before, had raged one of the bloodiest sections of the Somme attacks, and during one year the whole place had been a forgotten corner of our back areas. It seemed odd and a little discouraging to be back again in the old trenches where the Ulstermen had fought in 1916, as though so much blood and effort had been wasted. However we soon had the impression that we were not destined to spend much longer there. In Nomansland the outlines of old orchards indicated the former site of the village of Hamel, on our immediate right was the swampy wood of Aveluy, and as the month of August wore on the enemy gradually evacuated his part of the wood and drew in his outpost line in the Ancre valley round Hamel.

Our Brigade headquarters were in cupola shelters in a sunken road west of Englebelmer, and so far as I remember half my observers were perched in a crow's nest in a high tree close by. From it and another observation post which I had, one could see constant traffic on a road which ran alongside the Ancre for a couple of miles, and in the side of the same road, between Beaucourt, Miraumont and Irles, many dugouts. Eventually this road must have been effectively harassed by our artillery, for when I passed along it after the enemy's withdrawal it was littered with derelict wagons and dead horses. On August 18th when our Brigade crossed the Ancre in the wake of the retreating enemy, I was on leave, thus missing an action of the Brigade for the first and last time, and, on returning from leave on the 25th, found that owing to the comparative rapidity of our advance and the desolate nature of the old Somme battlefield the back area authorities could give no information as to the direction my Division had taken.

Eventually having reached our old front line in a succession of lorries I struck the Miraumont road—already referred to, and by a lucky accident found our Brigade transport lines. Next day I joined Brigade headquarters in a German artillery dugout west of the main road connecting Le Sars and Courcelette, presumably on the 28th as the 62nd Brigade had already taken Le Sars and the Division had pushed forward east of the Le Bargue–Eaucourt road.

CHAPTER XIII

THE BEGINNING OF THE END
(SEE MAP FACING PAGE 95)

THE first action after my return was a big advance by the Brigade eastwards across the Ligny–Thilloy–Flers road in the direction of Beaulencourt. We had moved our headquarters the previous night to the curious mound, honeycombed with dugouts, called the Butte de Warlencourt, and while the advance was taking place it was again moved forward to an open trench just west of the spot called Luisenhof Farm. The term " Brigade Headquarters " except in static trench warfare, always meant as regards personnel, the Brigadier, Brigade Major, Signal officer and myself with about fifty men, mostly signallers and runners. The Staff Captain and any attached officers usually made the transport lines their base, and from there managed supplies, the routine office work and the considerable administrative side of a Brigade.

I think it was at this time—unless the incident occurred two years earlier in the same country—that I spent ten minutes with an artillery observing officer, who having no particular target in view amused himself by " sniping " with his 18-pounder guns first one and then another solitary German walking across a field. One derived, I regret to remember, a primitive thrill from watching this expensive game and the growing nervousness of the pedestrians as they gradually realized that the shells were following them until they ran for their lives and disappeared into a wood.

The attack on the strongly-held village of Beaulencourt on September 1st gave a striking proof of the enormous advance made by the new British Army in the technique of warfare, for it was a small masterpiece achieved with one tenth of the casualties it would assuredly have cost us in 1916. The long western-front of the village, which appeared the main line of approach, was defended by numerous well-concealed pits for riflemen and machine-guns, and had we been attacking in the 1916 method the course of events would probably have been as follows. A tremendous artillery bombardment, perhaps for two days, would have annihilated the village and churned up the ground, and at zero hour our troops would have advanced in waves across the belt of land commanded by the various posts, who, as our barrage passed on behind them, would have opened a murderous direct fire on them and taken an enormous toll in casualties. Very possibly we should never have reached the village, but consolidated a line of shell-holes a few hundred yards beyond the starting-point, from which a fresh attack would have been delivered perhaps several days later, and a communiqué would doubtless have said "We gained so many yards on such and such a front, inflicting numerous casualties on the enemy".

By September, 1918, however we had acquired an improved technique. The Western side of the village was left severely alone, and the attack was arranged for the northern end of the village, a procedure which involved in itself a movement and assembly by night that would have been difficult for inexperienced officers. The artillery fired numerous periodic "crashes", and their support at zero was arranged to appear merely a repetition of one of these and did not specially indicate the time or direction of the attack. Under cover of complete darkness the village was rushed and the defences taken in the rear, the whole affair being a complete surprise. One hundred and thirty-three unwounded prisoners, two field guns and nine anti-tank guns (enormous rifles mounted on stands), and no less than thirty-six machine guns were taken, besides a well-equipped hospital with a hundred and one beds. It is very important to remember that the artillery had improved their technique just as had the staffs and the infantry: in 1916 one could hardly have relied on the accuracy and exact synchronization, which one had now learned to expect, required for such an operation.

Visiting the village about dawn I encountered a German, who bolted out of a hole as I was approaching, and brought him back with me in triumph, and the episode ultimately reached Corps headquarters in the form that "a Brigade Staff officer had captured a German general". So is history made. During a subsequent visit I struck on a German mortuary shed literally stacked with naked corpses streaked with vivid colours, while a few others were lying about outside—a gruesome and revolting spectacle.

On September 3rd the 42nd and 17th Divisions pushed forward on our flanks to Barastry and Rocquiqny, so that for a time we were squeezed out of the advance. The Germans indeed retired several miles before showing fight again, and the Brigade was not in action until the 10th. During this period we had moved on to the site of Sailly-Saillisel, a miserable collection of shell-holes and tree-stumps ont he Bapaume–Peronne road, where our bivouac under trench-shelters was rendered disagreeable by very heavy rains. From here we went on to Manancourt on the Canal du Nord, where the Germans had just been forced to retreat again. Having to ride back to Sailly-Saillisel to fetch my field-glasses which I had forgotten, I got overtaken by darkness amid the wilderness of old shell-holes, and finding it impossible even to lead my horse had to take the longer route by the main road, an incident illustrative of the state of that countryside.

I think it was that night while on my way that I watched a thrilling chase of a big German bombing-plane by one of our small fighting planes. The big machine, caught in the glare of several searchlights, tried in vain to dodge into obscurity, while from the small one above it came the rattle of machine-gun fire, like an angry insect worrying its prey. Suddenly a shower of lights began to fall and an instant later the big German 'plane began to drive earthwards in a long trail of flame. It was curious to hear the sound of cheering coming from various directions in the apparently uninhabited wilderness around one. The incident reminds me that one not uncommon sight by day in the later stages of the War was that of an observation balloon coming down in flames while the occupant descended in a parachute under machine-gun fire from the enemy aeroplane.

The Ytres–Manancourt canal, or Canal du Nord, where we had now arrived was the limit of the old Somme battlefield, and though all houses had been destroyed by the Germans in their retreat to the Hindenburg line in April, 1917, we were now again entering comparatively unspoilt country. At Manancourt we found comfortable and warm huts, evidently a former Corps headquarters. On the night of the 9–10th, which was dark and rainy, we relieved the 62nd Brigade in trenches just north-west of our old village of Epehy, which we had left in such different circumstances in March, and next day took over also the front of the 64th Brigade. We were now holding what had in the spring formed the reserve line of the Brigades which had been in those days on our left flank. Our headquarters were on the Fins–Nurlu road, in huts which we subsequently found to be marked on a captured German map as

THE BEGINNING OF THE END

a nest of battery positions. Battalion headquarters were in deep dugouts north of the railway between Fins and Heudicourt.

At 9.30 a.m. on the 13th a ragged-looking deserter arrived in front of our headquarters with an escort, and, as soon as he was addressed in German, explained eagerly that he had come over in order to avoid taking part in an attack with " flammenwerfer " on a part of our line called Chapel Hill, which he said was to take place at 10 a.m. It speaks well for the organization of our artillery that at the exact moment indicated our batteries were able to put down a barrage so effective that the attack only resulted in the loss by the attackers themselves of a machine-gun and ten prisoners.

On the night of the 15-16th the Brigade was relieved and went back to the Canal du Nord. Our headquarters were unfortunately in conspicuous tents on high ground west of Manancourt, and close to a sunken road, in which were other tents for our personnel of servants, runners and signallers. Our mess was in a large marquee, and we were sitting in it dining—without taking any precautions regarding lights—when at 9 p.m. we heard the ominous droning hum of an aeroplane. We blew out all the candles, but as the " hum-hum-hum " sounded just overhead a bomb came whistling down and crashed right in front of the door, knocking everything over and filling the tent with dust and smoke. Three more came sizzling down in rapid succession, two falling right in the sunken road, and as we came out into the open, amid groans and exclamations from all around, we surveyed an appalling scene. One bomb had fallen right on a tent occupied by the clerks, and the Brigade Major's sergeant clerk, who was also my own special clerk, had been literally blown in two. Five others had been killed, and ten wounded (including my own batman who had been with me since July, 1916), and others were suffering from shock, representing in all a loss of about thirty per cent. of our personnel.

In a unit where everyone was in some way a specialist, the extent of the disaster can be imagined. What made matters worse was that it took nearly an hour to get a doctor and an ambulance. Soon after the arrival of the latter a terrific storm arose which flooded the camp, sweeping away the Brigadier's tent, and about 4 a.m. a long-range high-velocity gun, which had normally been directed on the canal bridges, began to fire methodically at spots within a few hundred yards of us. We then moved our camp, but before this the Brigade Major had succeeded in writing out—our typewriter had been blown up—the orders for an attack which we had just received instructions for the Brigade to make on the 18th. It had been a very unpleasant night, but we could at least feel that only amazing good fortune had saved our mess tent from the first bomb, which was obviously meant for it, and dropped from a very low altitude.

The new attack, for which the Brigade Major had drafted the orders in circumstances so little favourable to clear thinking, was to be directed first to the recovery of what had been up to 21st March our own forward zone, and secondly to the capture of what had then been the German front line system. The first operation was entrusted to the 62nd Brigade, the latter to ourselves with the 64th Brigade on our left flank. On the 17th the troops moved forward, our headquarters passing the night with the 62nd Brigade staff in the very headquarters which that staff had been occupying on March 21st. Next morning, while the first attack was in progress, we moved our headquarters up to a dugout in a sunken road close to the old familiar railway-cutting and scarce fifteen-hundred yards north of Peizières-Epehy. Until March 21st this dugout had been the headquarters of a Battalion of the 62nd Brigade, and we found in it a regimental cheque-book and other papers lying on a shelf covered with the dust of six months.

The progress of the attack brought our troops back into parts of our old front line east of Epehy, and the 1st Wilts established their headquarters in the road called 14 Willows, and close to the trees from which the name was derived. It was thrilling to encounter our old trench notice-boards, " Poplar Trench ", etcetera, still in position. The situation was awkward as the 58th Division on our right had not been able to keep pace, but the Brigade was relieved on the 19th, and rested until the 24th in the

Manancourt area. We had taken four hundred and twenty-six prisoners, including no less than twenty officers, and eight field-guns.

The next field of operations was the area immediately on the left of that which we had just left on the 19th. The trenches which we took on September 25th from the 17th Division faced Gonnelieu and included a piece of scrub, Gauche Wood, which as a conspicuous landmark drew frequent shell-fire on the troops holding it. Our Brigade headquarters were in a solitary dugout on an eminence called Chapel Hill, at which the enemy fired gas-shells every evening. We made an attack which was only partially successful on the 29th, and I remember a walk, accompanied by a major from the 6th Battalion, over the great height north of Gonnelieu known as Fusilier Ridge, where there was some liveliness due to enemy snipers, and where we found a very fatigued Colonel sitting in a shallow front-line trench who, when asked for information, spoke with great contempt of the official version of his Brigade's dispositions, a version which appeared to be optimistic. Nevertheless, the enemy on about the 30th effected a complete retirement to the Honnecourt–Banteux canal, whither we followed him, moving our own headquarters to a quarry on the road from Gouzeaucourt to Villers-Guislain. Our front line was now what had been in 1917 the British front line overlooking the canal, but from December, 1917, until March 21st, had been the German support line. We heard at this time that a British tank had been blown up on a mine-field (rows of trench-mortar bombs buried in pairs with intervals of a few feet between pairs), laid by ourselves before March 21st to catch German tanks. Another incident I remember was finding behind a hedge near Villers-Guislain a German battery with the gun-teams lying dead beside their guns. I think the 6th Leicesters had taken these pieces.

For some days we sat facing the enemy across the canal, patrols seeking every night to find a crossing. I remember only the high road from Gonnelieu running steeply down into the ruins of Banteux where our foremost posts, belonging to the 7th Leicestershires, lay among the ruined houses. On October 5th the enemy retired again. The troops on our right were first over the canal, at Honnecourt: we ourselves crossed at 10 a.m. by the remains of the broken bridges, and by noon had occupied without opposition the old Hindenburg line, the same area I had studied so often through the telescope before March 21st. By the evening we had established our headquarters in the Hindenburg line, and orders were given for a complicated attack on the next line, the Beaurevoir system. The scheme, which once more illustrated the improvement in tactical method since 1916, comprised an easterly attack by the 1st Wilts, who were to capture a road and trenches east of Montecouvez Farm, and an attack swinging northwards by the two remaining battalions, who were to form up and start from a line indicated

K

in the area which had first to be taken by the 1st Wilts.

On the evening of the 7th October our headquarters moved round Vaucelles Wood and occupied a solitary old house known as Gratte Panche Farm—in the middle of a field. It was complete with roof and windows, the first tangible proof that we were entering the promised land beyond all the devastated areas. It was a pitch-dark night, and I remember marvelling at the manner in which the Wiltshires found their way to their starting point and were formed up ready to attack by 1 a.m. Before 3 a.m. batches of prisoners were already arriving, and I was busy examining them till at 4.30 a.m. I was ordered to go forward and see the 6th and 7th Leicesters forming up in the area just taken by the Wiltshires and in the slang of the period " jumping off ".

As their zero hour was to be 5 a.m. there was no time to be lost. The German batteries must have been well behind the line, for they were now very active, and as I entered Montecouvez Farm—in reality a small village—falling shells and a shower of bombs from a low-flying aeroplane combined to produce a terrifying uproar. Houses were crashing and bricks flying in every direction, always a specially unpleasant sound in the darkness, and I ran hard through the village and on along a road which brought me to the positions just taken by the Wiltshires. From the spot where the trenches they had captured

THE BEGINNING OF THE END 147

crossed this road, there was another road running north to the assembly positions of the other two battalions, and following this, visiting the Company commanders on the way, I found the attacking waves of the two battalions already moving forward towards Ardissart Farm. Day dawned, enabling me to watch their progress, and having carried out my instructions I started to return by the same road, which proved difficult as it was being swept by enemy machine-guns which were still holding out in Angle Château and harassing the whole area. I found the Wilts Battalion headquarters sitting under heavy shell-fire in the road just north of Montecouvez Farm, a road which had appeared from the map to be sunken, but turned out to have a low bank on one side only. I was back at headquarters by 7 a.m., with a good appetite and a report that the complicated operation had been crowned with complete success, and we eventually learned that four field-guns, sixty-seven machine-guns, six trench-mortars and six hundred and twenty-four prisoners had fallen to the Brigade. Our enthusiasm was damped by an astonishing order to make a fresh attack the same evening, but vehement protests from the Brigadier—who was always ready to risk unpopularity in high quarters when he felt his duty to his subordinates demanded it—led to this order being cancelled.

CHAPTER XIV

THE LAST PHASE

THE enemy now effected another large retirement, evacuating, for the first time since our attack at Cambrai, villages not merely intact but full of civilians who had been under German rule since 1914, and for the next ten days we lived in one of these villages, Caullery by name, though for a couple of days we had had our headquarters in a dugout near Montecouvez Farm. The effect on the spirits of the troops of seeing civilians and feeling that the enemy was at last beginning to break was instantaneous, and I remember the delight of a column of troops marching along a road when I galloped back over the fields from the village of Walincourt wearing a battered top hat I had picked up. Unfortunately the area of comfortable billets we had been given for the Brigade was very considerably reduced by the arrival in a procession of motor-cars and lorries of our Corps headquarters, who took over a large slice of our billets. As we understood that they had remained since August 18th in their old summer headquarters, till they ended by being many miles behind the infantry, it was suggested that they had waited to learn, as

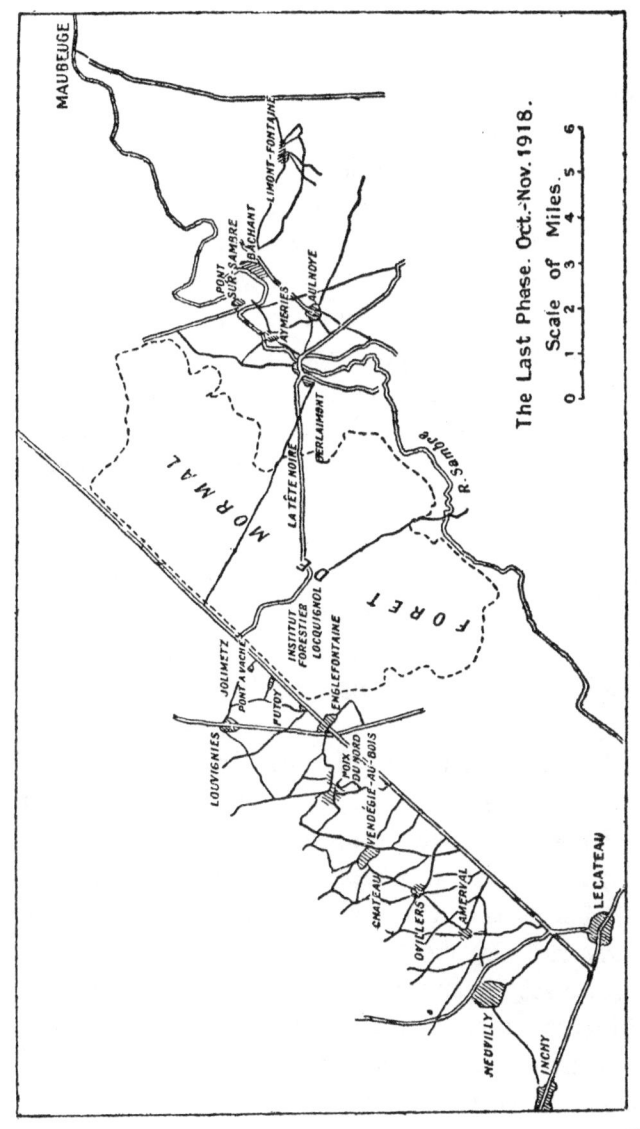

each successive area was recaptured, whether comfortable quarters were available. There was also some interference with the ration-supply on account of the large demand on the available supply of transport to facilitate this migration.

We stayed in Caullery till October 22nd. On that day we marched up through Inchy to Neuvilly, a small town lying on a river midway between Solesmes to the north and Le Cateau to the south. The 52nd Brigade had established their line across the river and just east of Neuvilly, and beyond lay a great rolling country with few woods but covered in places with standing crops. Our rôle was to take over from the 52nd Brigade, and execute a long sweeping advance in a north-easterly direction to Vendegies au Bois. Visiting their battalions on the 22nd I was struck by their bedraggled appearance, for they had been exposed without shelter to very heavy rain, the Colonel and adjutant of one battalion sitting in a ditch, under the shelter of a waterproof sheet, from which they had to crawl out. In the town itself I conferred with the Brigade staff and also found a cellar for our own headquarters. The walls were literally covered with sleepy flies, but it was the best available, as the less shelled parts of the town were already full of artillery.

In the area between Neuvilly and the German-held Ovillers were several parallel roads running more or less north to south, on one of which the 1st Wilts and 7th Leicesters were to form up for the attack,

THE LAST PHASE 151

which was to take place at two o'clock in the morning. Some instinct led the enemy to lay a violent barrage on this very road just before that hour, and Maclaren the Adjutant of the 7th Battalion, was killed by a shell at the corner of a little orchard. Nevertheless the Battalions cleared the area, the 6th Leicesters assisting on the line east of Ovillers, and the latter battalion according to plan continued the advance towards Vendegies at 7.15 a.m. One company worked round the wood which lay in front of Vendegies Château and took it in flank, capturing the German regimental commander. The latter said he had gone below to avoid a crash of shells, and that " When I came out again, Tommy was in the garden ".

Between 10 and 11 a.m. the 62nd Brigade had passed through us and in their turn continued the advance beyond Vendegies. Our headquarters, after a temporary halt at a copse east of Amerval, moved into Ovillers, and from thence early next morning (the 24th) into Vendegies Château, where at 9 a.m. we received news that the 62nd Brigade had occupied the town of Poix du Nord. The Brigadier in an optimistic mood decided to establish his headquarters there, and we rode to the spinning factory (a great chimney tower and building at the west entrance), from whence the signal officer and I went on into the town to look for a suitable headquarters. We felt a certain thrill in entering a comparatively large town and being greeted in every house by groups of excited civilians with delirious enthusiasm and offers of coffee, and by 9 a.m. we had established our headquarters in a suitable house. Unfortunately the advance had been checked on the eastern outskirts of the town, and as we were having our third coffee the mutual enthusiasm was damped by vigorous bursts of shelling up and down the street where we had selected our new headquarters. One shell hit the back part of our house, and an old man who had been lying there bedridden for many years emerged from the debris, apparently cured. So at least we said, I cannot now remember how far we were embellishing the incident. Our excessive optimism had resulted in the establishment of a Brigade headquarters considerably in advance of its battalions, so by 3 p.m. we had returned rather crestfallen to Vendegies Château.

On the 26th the Division was relieved, and our Brigade had a few days' rest round Ovillers. Riding back to Neuvilly, the Divisional headquarters, I passed several dead soldiers of the Brigade we had relieved four days earlier, lying in a frequented road outside Neuvilly, and remember our Brigadier to whom I reported the incident, telephoning to the Divisional Staff, " I hear you have dead men outside your headquarters ". The episode is curiously suggestive of the atmosphere of war.

On the 29th-30th we relieved the 52nd Brigade at Poix du Nord, taking over their Brigade headquarters in a large brewery, combined with the owner's dwelling, in the centre of the town. We occupied basement cellars, in which we were in Sir Thomas More's phrase " rather secure than safe ", since we could distinctly hear every shell which entered the town. That same night the enemy put down a heavy artillery " counter-preparation ", doubtless anticipating a resumption of our advance, and from midnight to 4.30 a.m. a stream of shells, at least a thousand, came whistling over amid an unceasing clatter of falling bricks. Unfortunately the bulk of the civilian population of the town were still there, and apart from the danger of ordinary shell-fire, were exposed without equipment to gas. On one occasion while we were there, being caught in a street by a burst of shelling I dived into a cellar which was full of civilians. Noticing that some of the shells were gas I donned my gas-mask, when I became self-conscious on realizing that my civilian companions were helpless, and made a dash for home. Some French lorries arrived presently with gas-masks for the civilians, many of whom also were evacuated, but I think there must have been a good many casualties. An interpreter told me six hundred were gassed. It must have been at this time that a regimental officer, I fancy an adjutant, who was established with his group in a brick cottage at a cross-roads in the fields, with a sand-bagged shelter behind it, explained to me, when I suggested that the house was a rather dangerous location, that there was always time to dodge round to the shelter when there was any shelling, and in fact we both performed this manœuvre a minute later to avoid a couple of salvos. I remember remarking to him as I took my leave soon after that I hoped he would not do it once too often, and when I returned to my headquarters the first thing I heard was that he had been hit while running round the house to cover.

The last act of the long drama was now opening, though I confess I did not believe it to be so at the time for one had grown so accustomed to the routine of war that the military habit of mind had become almost a second nature. The period now approaching its climax had been one of strenuous activity. Many of our troops had been " over the top " four or five times in a couple of months, many too were men who had been wounded and returned to duty two or three times. It was about this time that one morning when the Battalion Commanders were conferring with the Brigadier, myself acting as secretary, a luxurious car drove up and an eminent general came in. As we stood up he shouted that the Irish mail boat had been sunk, that the Brigade had taken too many prisoners lately, and he didn't want so many in future! As he clattered out again, the Brigadier observed without comment, " Let me see—where were we, gentlemen ? "

On the 3rd November we were relieved and returned to Ovillers, but the same day received orders that the 3rd, 4th and 5th British Armies were to resume the offensive the following day in conjunction with the 4th French Army. On our particular sector the 17th Division who were actually in the line in front of Poix were to advance towards their right flank into the great Forest of Mormal, and our Division was to pass through them and continue the advance towards the Sambre.

On the 4th November accordingly we moved up through Poix and Futoy along the main road to Pont-à-Vache, where we spent the night. I remember being shocked on the way by the sight of the body of a small girl mangled by a shell, lying by the roadside between Futoy and Pont-à-Vache. At 6 a.m. on the 5th our Division was marching east towards the Forêt de Mormal, by 8.30 we were at the " Institut Forestier " in the heart of the forest ; and by 11.30 had emerged on the further side and established ourselves in the village of " La Tete Noire ". This unopposed passage through the forest, which even a few machine-guns could have converted into a formidable obstacle, was a welcome surprise and confirmed the tales we now began to hear from civilians of the growing discouragement and disorder in the ranks of the retreating army.

Great slices of the forest had been denuded of timber to provide trench material, and the Socialist doctor of Berlaimont, a town we were then approaching, told me a curious story of how when the Germans began their wood-cutting operations some seven or eight months after the Mons retreat, they discovered two companies of British infantry who, cut off during the retreat, had managed to survive in the heart of the forest, with the help of regular supplies from the surrounding country folk, none of whom betrayed the secret. There were many dramatic tales of other French or British stragglers, who were looked after for years by the local people, some going about openly in civilian dress, others remaining always indoors and hiding in great baking ovens when the houses where they were sheltered were raided. A French engineer officer had lived for two years at Berlaimont, till he set off one day to rejoin his army, and a private soldier was still there when we arrived. An amusing relic of the occupation was an order I was shown stating the amount of fine which would be levied on those whose hens did not furnish the required quota of eggs for the army of occupation.

Between November 4th and 6th our problem was to get across the Sambre and drive across the area south of Maubeuge. The 62nd Brigade had entered the riverside town of Berlaimont where they found enemy rearguards disputing the river-crossings, but on the night of the 5th they constructed rough bridge-heads, by means of which our Brigade got across early in the morning of the 6th, and cleared the suburbs on the opposite bank. Our headquarters had been established in a house on the western outskirts of Berlaimont, and during the afternoon I crossed the river with the Brigade Major and passing along the tow-path turned east through the suburb of Aulnoye and visited our battalions. We were returning and had just reached the riverside when a sudden hurricane of shells came down round us, and dashing into a small house we hurled ourselves into a cellar to the consternation of an old lady who believed the Germans had returned. Emerging after about five minutes to sprint along the bank we passed new shell-holes right across the track which made us thankful we had taken shelter in time.

As day broke on November 7th the advance was resumed—as it turned out, for the last time. Our objectives were, first the high ground west of Limont-Fontaine, then the Maubeuge-Avesnes road and Beaufort village. The "clearing-up" of Aulnoye had been delayed through a humane decision not to employ on that inhabited area the usual artillery barrage. The first objective was taken with ease, the 6th Brigade passed through us to establish the Second, and about 7 a.m. I rode to the village of Bacchant, by way of Aulnoye station and Quatre Bras cross roads, with a major of the 6th Leicesters, and finally waited for Brigade headquartars at Etree, a western suburb of Bacchant. In the afternoon as I was walking round the main square of Bacchant with the Brigade Major to visit the three Battalions' headquarters, a few desultory shells came over, and the last the Brigade was destined to hear.

That evening the 17th Division came through us and we withdrew to rest at Berlaimont. Three days later—at a moment when we were elaborating plans for a fresh advance, a signaller handed me a telegram informing us that hostilities would cease at 11 a.m. Despite all the portents we had had of an impending collapse, we had grown so accustomed to the routine of war that the news did not excite any of the emotion it would have done in the earlier years, and I can still remember the polite smile with which our serjeant-clerk read the order.

This mood, and the atmosphere of a large French village, made impossible any counterpart to the delirious scenes which, as we heard later, took place in London. The officers of one of our battalions which I visited in the evening celebrated the event with a convivial, though not unduly riotous, gathering, except perhaps for certain destruction caused by a horse which some of us led through a chemist's shop to visit a major who had, we thought, gone to bed too early.

Looking back through this account after a lapse of ten years I can find little to add in the way of comment or narrative. Having never at any time in the War fallen victim to the hysterical anti-Germanism of the period or to the delusion that any class could derive permanent benefit from such a struggle, I have nothing to retract and no revulsion of feeling to express. Furthermore, when the War came I was old enough to escape the neurosis and loss of the sense of proportion which has been its inevitable aftermath for some of those whose misfortune it was to be flung straight from school into the fighting-line. I cannot help feeling, however, that the simple statement of the events described in these pages is as good testimony to the awful conditions as could be found in any novel, but the only conclusion I wish to draw explicitly from it is that future generations should recognise the patient, unostentatious gallantry with which our men discharged their duty through those weary yet heroic years.

One who has read this manuscript informs me that I give the impression that our Army was badly led, that the French and the Germans were better off than we in this respect. The question is not so simple. Our professional officers, with certain defects and virtues which they shared with most other Englishmen, were inferior to none, but they were totally inadequate, both in numbers and staff experience for the work of handling millions of men. Why should one expect a man who had never commanded more than a Battalion to make no mistakes in charge of a Division or a Corps? Our regimental officers—almost all civilians—bore a much heavier burden of leadership, owing largely to the absence of regular N.C.O.'s, than their German or French colleagues and acquitted themselves magnificently; our Supply Service was the envy of all foreigners who came in contact with us, our gunners acquired an amazing technical efficiency, and our airmen real superiority, and our whole achievement must remain for ever the greatest triumph of amateur genius and improvisation in history. After all, perhaps the most convincing epitaph of the British Army is the map which forms the frontispiece to this narrative, with its concentration of German Divisions in front of our attacking forces. *Fas est et ab hoste doceri.*

www.ingramcontent.com/pod-product-compliance
Lightning Source LLC
Chambersburg PA
CBHW031146160426
43193CB00008B/265